DECORATING IDEAS
for the HOME

DECORATING
IDEAS
for the
HOME

Inspirational solutions for every room

MIKE LAWRENCE and JAN EATON

Sebastian Kelly

Paperback edition published by
Sebastian Kelly
2 Rectory Road, Oxford, OX4 1BW

Produced by Anness Publishing Limited
Hermes House, 88-89 Blackfriars Road
London SE1 8HA

ISBN 1-84081-085-8

A CIP catalogue record for this book is available from the British Library

Publisher: Joanna Lorenz
Managing Editor: Judith Simons
Designer: Michael Morey
Photographer: John Freeman
Illustrator: Andrew Green
Soft Furnishings section by Jan Eaton

Also published as *Great Home Decorating Ideas*

Printed and bound in Singapore by Star Standard Industries Pte. Ltd.

PUBLISHER'S NOTE
The author and publishers have made every effort to ensure that all instructions
contained within this book are accurate and safe, and cannot accept liability for
any resulting injury, damage or loss to persons or property however it may arise.
If in any doubt as to the correct procedure to follow for any home improvements
task, seek professional advice.

The publishers would like to thank Jan Eaton for
devising and writing the Soft Furnishings section and
Fiona Skrine for devising and demonstrating the special paint effects on pages 22-7.

The publishers would also like to thank the following
companies for their kind permission to reproduce the
following pictures in this book.

t = top; b = bottom; c = centre; l = left; r = right

Addis Ltd: page 59 cl.
The Amtico Company Ltd: page 37 br.
Laura Ashley: pages 48 tl, 58 br, 76 t, 78 r, 81 br,
    84 bl, 93 br.
Richard Burbidge Ltd: pages 12, 48-9.
Castelnau Tiles: pages 36 br, 47 tr.
Concord Lighting Ltd: pages 62 b, 63 cl cr b, 67 tl b,
    68 r, 69 bc br.

Corres Mexican Tiles: page 34 cr.
Cliffhanger Shelving Systems: pages 58 tl, 59 tr.
Crown Paints: pages 20 tr cr, 30-1, 31 cr br.
Cuprinol Ltd: pages 21 bl br, 43 h.
Dulux: pages 6, 8b, 9 tl, 13 tr, 14 tr, 18-19, 18, 19,
    20 tl, 21 t, 46, 48 b, 79 br, 88 bl, 98 b.
Cristal (H & R Johnson Tiles) Ltd: pages 10 b, 34 bl,
    61 tr.
Crucial Trading Ltd: page 41 b.
Fired Earth Tiles plc: pages 34 tr, 35, 36 t bl.
Fireplace Designers Ltd: page 47 tl.
Forbo-CP (Fablon) Ltd: pages 8 t, 66, 28 b, 30 l,
    31 bl, 49 b.
Forbo-Kingfisher Ltd: pages 10 t, 28 t, 29 t, 89 tr.
Forbo-Nairn Ltd: pages 37 t, 41 tr, 42 t.
Harlequin Wallcoverings Ltd: pages 13 tl, 29 b, 48 b,
    85 t, 86 br.

Harrison Drape: pages 13 b, 74 t, 75 t.
Hayloft Woodwork: pages 8 b, 98 t.
Heuga: page 41 tl.
Junckers Ltd: pages 11 b, 65 cr, 42 b, 43 t.
Kevin MacPartland: page 49 tr.
Mazda Lighting: pages 62 t, 63 t, 64, 65 tl tr cl, 67 tr,
    68 l, 69 t bl.
MFI: pages 9 tr, 11 t, 58 bl, 61 tl.
Monkwell Fabrics and Wallpapers: page 15 b.
Mr Tomkinson: page 40.
Sanderson: pages 14 tr b, 80 t, 92 t.
Muriel Short Designs: page 87 br.
Silver Lynx Products: page 99 c.
Spur Shelving Ltd: pages 97 b, 99 b.
Today Interiors: pages 15 t, 70.
Wicanders: pages 37 cr, 42 c.
Elizabeth Whiting and Associates: page 83 br.

CONTENTS

DECORATING
DECISIONS

The hardest part of home decoration is deciding precisely what is wanted and planning how to achieve it. The decision may simply involve redecoration of walls and floors, with a new choice of colour or pattern, or may be more complex, perhaps involving major changes to the style, layout, features and fittings of a room or rooms.

For example, it may seem likely that better use can be made of the interior space that is available. An easy way of doing this is to rearrange or change some of the furniture, whether it is freestanding or built-in – but a more radical approach may bring even more dramatic gains. Partitioning some rooms, linking others, even changing the use to which individual rooms have previously been put, can revolutionize the way a home works. This approach is particularly relevant as the occupants' needs alter over the years, since a house that worked well with young children will not suit a family with teenagers, and once the children have flown the nest their parents will want to use the house in a different way again.

On a smaller scale, even the way in which individual rooms are decorated and furnished can have a major effect on the way they look and feel. Many people find that achieving the style they want is often a process of evolution rather than revolution; few people can get everything right first time. The secret of success lies in understanding the basic rules of colour scheming and in learning how to make the best use of the wide range of materials and techniques available to the interior designer today. Lighting can transform an interior, too, and guidance is given on your choices here.

Lastly, it also means taking a close look at what soft furnishings can contribute to the scheme. New curtains, covers and cushions in bright and complementary colours can give instant life to a room without major upheaval and expense. Simple techniques for making your own soft furnishings are included in the last section of this book.

OPPOSITE
The art of successful decoration lies in marrying materials that protect and enhance the various surfaces around the home with a touch of decorative flair and originality that will give every room a style all its own and reflect the owner's personal taste and lifestyle.

MAKING AN ASSESSMENT

The best way to get an objective view of a home's interior condition is to imagine that it is up for sale and to view it in the role of a prospective purchaser. The aim of the exercise is not to give rise to a severe bout of depression, but to make it clear what exists in the home and what could be done to change or improve it.

Start at the front door, and step into the hallway. Is it bright and well lit, or gloomy and unwelcoming? A lighter colour scheme could make a narrow room appear more spacious, and better lighting would make it seem more inviting. Decorating the wall opposite the front door would make a long hall appear shorter, while changing the way the staircase is decorated could make it a less – or more – dominant feature. Is the staircase well lit, for safety's sake as well as for looks? Opening up the space beneath the stairs could get rid of what

ABOVE Choose an integrated decorating scheme for hallways, stairs and landing areas. Bring down the apparent ceiling height using a dado (chair) rail or decorative border.

BELOW The living room has to be light and airy during the day, yet cosy and comfortable in the evening. The fireplace and a central table provide the main focal points here.

is typically an untidy gloryhole (storage room), taking up space without saving any. Lastly, are the wall and floor coverings practical? The hall floor is bound to be well trodden, and needs to be durable and easy to clean as well as looking attractive.

Now move into the main living room. This is always the most difficult room in the house to decorate and furnish successfully because of its dual purpose. It is used both for daily life and to entertain visitors. It must be fresh and lively by day, yet cosy and peaceful in the evening. One of the chief keys to success is flexible lighting that can be altered to suit the room's different uses, but the decorations and furnishings all have their part to play too.

Look at the colour scheme. How well does it blend in with the furnishings, the curtains and drapes, the floor covering? Are there any interesting features such as a fireplace, an alcove, an archway into another room, even an ornate cornice around the ceiling? Some might benefit from being highlighted, other less attractive ones would be better disguised.

Next, examine how the room works. Are traffic routes congested? Are the seating arrangements flexible? Are there surfaces where things can easily be put down? Does any storage or display provision look good and work well? Can everyone who is seated see the television? Does everyone want to? Assessing the room in this way reveals its successes and failures, and shows how to eliminate the latter.

Continue the guided tour with the dining room – or dining area, if it is part of a through room. This is often the least used room in the house, so its design tends to be neglected. Since it is usually used for just one purpose –

eating – it needs to be decorated in a way that avoids visual indigestion. Warm, welcoming colour schemes and flexible lighting work best in this location; strident patterns and harsh colours are to be avoided.

Now turn to the kitchen. Whatever type of room it is, the most important thing is that it should be hygienic, for obvious reasons. Are the various surfaces in the room easy to keep clean, and to redecorate when necessary? Are there dust and grease traps? Is the lighting over the hob (burners) and counter tops adequate? Is the floor covering a practical choice? Since the kitchen is often the hub of family life, it needs to be functional but adaptable, and also pleasant to be in so that the cook does not mind the time spent slaving over a hot stove.

Bathrooms have their own special requirements, mainly revolving around combining comfort with a degree of waterproofing, especially if there are young children in the family. Are the decorations and floor covering suitable? How do they complement the bathroom suite? What about the space available within the room? Could congestion be relieved by moving

things around? – or by moving them out altogether: having a shower instead of a bath could create lots of extra space. Could a second bathroom be created elsewhere in the house? Otherwise, putting washbasins in some of the bedrooms could take the pressure off the family bathroom during the morning rush hour.

Lastly, bedrooms. In most, the bed is the focal point of the room, so the way it is dressed will be the main influence on the room's appearance. The colour scheme also has its part to play in making the room look comfortable and relaxing; remember that the room's occupant will see it from two viewpoints – on entering, and from the bed – so take this into account when assessing it. What about the ceiling? In the one room where people actually spend some time staring at it, does it deserve something a little more adventurous than white paint? Is the floor covering warm to the touch of bare feet? In children's rooms, is it also capable of withstanding the occasional rough and tumble or a disaster with the finger paints? Lastly, is the lighting satisfactory? Most bedrooms need a combination of subdued general

lighting and brighter local task lighting for things such as reading in bed, putting on make-up or tackling school homework. Some changes may make the room work a great deal more satisfactorily.

Once the tour of the house is complete there should be a clear picture of its condition and how well it works; and some ideas as to how it might be improved. Above all, it will have been viewed as a whole, not just as a series of individual rooms. That is the first step towards creating an attractive, stylish and above all practical home.

REORGANIZING SPACE

If a home does not function well, there are three choices. Two of these are thoroughly defeatist and may also be impractical: learn to live with it, or move to a more suitable house. The third is much more positive; alter it so that it gives the extra living space and the additional features needed.

The average home is basically a box, within which internal partitions create individual rooms, doors allow movement and windows let in light and air. Various services are included within the structure – heating, plumbing, wiring and so on. All these features can be altered, within reason, to make them work better.

When planning alterations, there are two considerations which should constantly be borne in mind. Are the changes feasible? And are they legal? It is essential to check with the local planning (zoning) and building control bodies to find out whether the work requires official approval.

Where to improve
Alterations to the use of space in the home are of two kinds. The first is to create new living space. The second is to alter the present layout of the interior and to change or improve the services. Here are some of the possibilities.

In the attic, unused space beneath a pitched roof could well become valuable extra living space. Remember, though, that providing access to the new rooms will mean losing some space on the floor below.

In the existing upstairs rooms, rearranging internal walls could create an extra bedroom or bathroom, while providing plumbing facilities in bedrooms could ease the pressure on the existing bathroom.

ABOVE Subdividing large rooms can help to create more effective use of space, by redefining traffic zones and providing more wall space for furniture.

LEFT Bathing facilities are often over-stretched, especially in family homes. Finding space for an extra shower cubicle can greatly relieve the traffic jams.

Downstairs, removing dividing walls to create large through rooms or partitioning large rooms to create two smaller ones, moving doorways to improve traffic flow, or altering the kitchen layout could all be considered. It might even be possible to turn an integral garage into extra living space.

Look at the possibility of changing the use to which individual rooms are

CONVERTING AN ATTIC

A full-scale conversion into one or more habitable rooms – that is, bedrooms and the like rather than just play or hobby space – is one of the biggest and most complex indoor home improvement projects. It involves altering the roof structure to make space for the rooms, strengthening the existing attic floor, providing access from the floor below, installing roof or dormer windows and extending existing services into the new rooms. Professional advice is needed here, and it is advisable to hand over the main structural alterations to a builder or specialist conversion firm. That still leaves plenty of scope for do-it-yourself finishing and fitting of the new rooms.

In many older homes, the space beneath a pitched (sloping) roof can be used to provide valuable extra living space, often with spectacular results.

put, especially if the family is increasing or decreasing in size. Reorganization can bring dramatic improvements to the way the house works.

Creating a through room

Creating a through room means removing an existing dividing wall, and may also require the repositioning of existing doorways and the formation of new windows. If the existing wall is loadbearing, a steel beam will have to be installed to carry the load, and lintels will also be needed over new windows and over new doors in other loadbearing walls. It may be necessary to reroute existing plumbing and electrical services that cross the wall that will be removed. Once the new opening has been formed, there will be extensive replastering to be done, and the floors in the two rooms will have to be linked smoothly. The original colour schemes of the two rooms will also probably be different, which may entail complete redecoration.

Partitioning an existing room

Subdividing an existing room into two smaller ones means building a new wall, possibly adding a door or window to one of the new rooms, and perhaps altering or extending existing plumbing, heating and electrical services to serve the two separate rooms.

The new dividing wall will generally be built as a timber-framed partition wall faced with plasterboard (gypsum board), but a solid blockwork wall could be built on suitable foundations, which may well need to be inserted.

Creating a new door opening

If the new opening is to be made in a loadbearing wall, a lintel must be used to bridge the opening. However, if the wall is a non-loadbearing partition, simple alterations to the wall framing are all that will be needed. The job will also involve some replastering work, making alterations to skirtings (baseboards) and floor surfaces, the fitting of architraves (trims) around the opening, and possibly alterations to existing plumbing, heating and electrical services if pipes or cables cross the area where the door will be installed.

Altering the kitchen layout

The amount of work depends on how extensive the rearrangement will be. At the very least there will be new base and wall units (cabinets) and counter tops, and these will probably involve some work on wall and floor surfaces. If repositioning sinks, cookers (stoves), dishwashers and the like, there will have to be alterations to plumbing and electrical services.

USING COLOUR, PATTERN AND TEXTURE

After redesigning the house layout and reorganizing each room, the next task is to start planning the colour schemes. To do this successfully, it helps to understand the basics of colour theory, and how to use pattern and texture to good effect.

When putting a colour scheme together, a device called the *colour wheel* can be used to help plan the various decorative effects. All colours are made by mixing together varying proportions of the three *primary* colours – red, yellow and blue. Mixing them in pairs creates three new *secondary* colours, with red and yellow making orange, yellow and blue making green, and blue and red making violet. Imagine these six colours making up segments of a circle in the order red, orange, yellow, green, blue and violet. Mix adjacent pairs together again, and you create six *tertiary* colours – red/orange, orange/yellow, yellow/green, green/blue, blue/violet and violet/red. Adding these to the circle gives the basic colour wheel of twelve segments.

There is one more ingredient to add to these colours: colour intensity or tone. By adding different amounts of white or black, you can produce lighter or darker shades of the original colours in almost infinite variety. And you can also, of course, use white, black and varying shades of grey as colours in their own right.

On the wheel, the twelve colours split into two groups. The colours from violet/red round to yellow are known as *advancing* colours because they appear to make wall and ceiling surfaces look nearer to the viewer than they really are. They make a room seem warm and welcoming, but also smaller. The remaining colours are known as *receding* colours because they have the opposite

THE COLOUR WHEEL

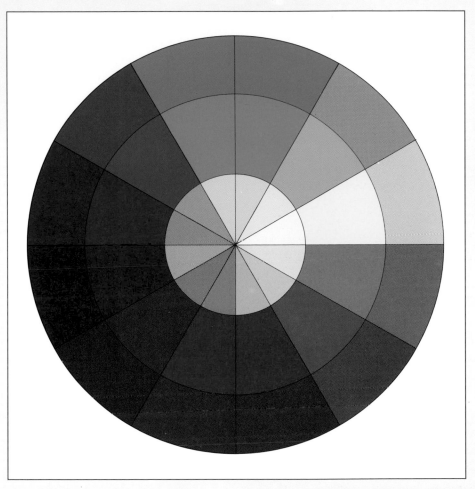

An understanding of colour and colour mixing will be invaluable when choosing a new colour scheme. The colour wheel is divided into 12 segments, and the central ring shows the primary, secondary and tertiary colours described in the text. The outer ring shows darker tones of these colours and the inner one lighter ones.

LEFT Blues, greys and plenty of white space create a cool, airy colour scheme that is the perfect complement for wooden fixtures and furnishings in a light shade of pine.

DECORATING DECISIONS

LEFT Blues and greens are naturally cool, receding colours, ideal for well-lit south-facing rooms, but can be warmed by splashes of contrast in orange and yellow.

ABOVE Neutral tones – beiges, creams and browns – create a colour scheme that is restful on the eye and can be teemed with almost any accessory shades.

visual effect, making a room look cool, and also larger than in reality. Which group is chosen as the basis for a colour scheme depends on the overall effect that is wanted in that particular room.

The colour wheel also helps to create colour *harmony* or *contrast*. Colours next to or near each other are said to be in colour harmony, giving a restful effect. However, too much colour harmony can become visually rather dull; it needs livening up with some elements of colour contrast, which come from using colours at opposite sides of the wheel. Colours exactly opposite each other, such as red and green, are called *complementary*. The ideal colour scheme is usually considered to be a basically harmonious one, with contrast added by the judicious use of contrasting or complementary colours for some elements of the design. Soft furnishings, such as scatter cushions or blinds and shades, chosen in a fabric to contrast with the overall colour scheme can add just the right amount of contrast to brighten up a room.

BELOW Nothing succeeds in creating a feeling of cosiness as well as the red/pink section of the colour wheel. Surface texture plays its part too, as does warm, natural wood fittings.

BELOW Bold splashes of colour can add interest and definition to a colour scheme that is basically neutral.

BELOW Wall coverings with a vertical pattern element can help to make rooms appear taller, but work well only when the walls are perfectly square.

ABOVE Small, random patterns are a better choice than larger motifs for small rooms, and are ideal for decorating areas where perfect pattern matching can be difficult.

Colour can also play tricks on the eye, which can be used to good effect in colour scheming. For example, painting a high ceiling in a dark colour makes it appear lower. The same effect applies on walls, where using dark colour on opposite walls makes a wide room seem narrower; conversely, using it on the end wall of a long, thin room and lighter colours on the side walls helps to make the room seem wider to the eye.

Using pattern

Pattern on walls, ceilings and floors adds visual interest to a colour scheme, either in harmony with the overall effect or to provide contrast – for example, by having a patterned wall covering on one wall, and the rest painted. Pattern as well as colour can cheat the eye and alter the apparent dimensions of a room. Wall coverings with a distinct horizontal pattern make walls seem wider and ceilings lower; strong vertical designs such as stripes have the opposite effect. The same applies to pattern in floor coverings, which can make a room look wider or narrower depending on which way the pattern element runs.

Pattern size has its own contribution to make. Wall and floor coverings with large pattern motifs make the surface they are on seem to advance and so make the room appear smaller, while tiny motifs have the opposite effect of making the surface appear to recede from the eye. Choosing patterned fabrics for cushions, curtains and drapes or bed linen is an ideal way of enlivening a decor with plain walls and woodwork.

LEFT Luxurious fabrics used for curtains, cushions and upholstery are often the ideal medium for adding patterned elements to a decor.

Using texture

Surface texture – in other words, a surface that is not completely smooth – helps to add variety and visual interest to your colour schemes. Wall coverings with a textured or embossed surface generally have a comparatively low relief which helps to soften the decorative effect of the material, while texture paints can be used to create effects that have quite a high relief and consequently look particularly striking when lit from the side. Textured finishes also have another benefit, of helping to disguise slightly irregular wall and ceiling surfaces.

RIGHT Sometimes richly textured upholstery and floor coverings benefit from the simplest of settings. Here textured walls and painted floorboards in pure white are the perfect backdrop.

EMBELLISHING WALLS AND FLOORS

Painting, paperhanging, tiling and laying floor coverings are the basic tools in the repertoire of any interior decorator. Modern paints and improvements in the design and manufacture of painting tools have made this element much less arduous than it was in the days of traditional oil-bound paints and distemper, and have made it possible for the amateur decorator to get professional-looking results every time. Special paint effects are also simple to achieve with basic know-how, and stencilling, marbling and rag-rolling can be an easy, dramatic and inexpensive alternative to wall coverings.

The term 'wall coverings' includes an enormous variety of designs, patterns and colourways, as well as textures and finishes. Careful selection and application is the key – and given the options, it should always be possible to find a covering to complement perfectly the atmosphere you are aiming to create.

Even more variety is available in tiling: as well as the traditional ceramic tile, which has been used in decorating for centuries, modern technology and innovation has produced vinyl, lino and cork, which offer a combination of properties that make them useful, practical alternatives in a wide range of situations, and which are generally much less expensive.

In carpeting, there is now a huge choice of colours and patterns in types and materials to suit all locations and wear conditions, available in a broad range of widths and sizes. Sheet vinyl comes in a similar range of colours and designs, with embossing to provide texture. Wooden floor covering is commonly available in two forms: wood block (sometimes known as wood mosaic), and wood strip.

All in all, the combinations and options open to the contemporary decorator are innumerable: the following section gives some guidelines on how to use them in the best and most effective way.

OPPOSITE
There is virtually no limit to the versatility of modern wall coverings. This complementary match of broken colour and simple stripes is linked by a striking multicoloured border at dado (chair) rail level.

TYPES OF PAINT, VARNISH AND STAIN

Paint works by forming a film on the surface to which it is applied. This film has to do three things: it must hide the surface underneath; it must protect it; and it must stay put. All paint has three main ingredients: pigment, binder and carrier. The *pigment* gives the film its colour and hiding power. The *binder* binds the pigment particles together into a continuous film as the paint dries, and also bonds the film to the surface beneath. In traditional paint this was a natural material such as linseed oil in oil paints, or glue size in distemper; but modern paints use synthetic resins such as alkyd, acrylic, vinyl and polyurethane. The third ingredient, the *carrier*, makes the paint flow smoothly as it is applied, and evaporates as the paint dries.

The ratio of pigment to binder in a paint affects the finish it has when it dries; the higher the pigment content, the duller the finish. By adjusting this ratio, paint manufacturers can produce paints that dry to a flat *matt* finish; to a silky sheen, *eggshell*; or to a high *gloss*. The choice depends on personal preference, tempered by the condition of the surface: high-gloss finishes highlight any imperfections, while matt finishes tend to disguise them.

Paint types

The paint types used in the home have different carriers. Water-based paint has the pigment and binder suspended in water as tiny droplets. It is an emulsion, like milk, and is usually called *emulsion* paint. (In the USA it is

ABOVE The yellow water-based paint chosen for the walls of this kitchen creates a basically warm colour scheme that is off-set by the gloss paint in cool colours selected for the woodwork. Solvent-based (oil) paint is ideal for surfaces which need washing down regularly.

LEFT There is nothing like a hint of strong contrast to bring a neutral colour scheme to life, as the bright red bedposts and picture rail do so dramatically here. Paints specially formulated for steamy locations should be used in en-suite bathrooms.

RIGHT Blues and greys are cool, fresh colours that particularly suit a well-lit children's room. The brightly painted ladder provides the perfect contrast. Painted surfaces need to be able to withstand some rough treatment in these locations.

Paint systems

A single coat of paint is too thin to form a durable paint film. To provide adequate cover and performance there must be a paint system consisting of several coats. What these are depends on the type of paint used, and on the surface being painted.

The first coat is a *sealer*, which is used where necessary to seal in things such as the natural resin in wood, or to prevent the paint from soaking into a porous surface.

The second is a *primer*, which provides a good key for the paint film to stick to. On metal surfaces, this also stops the metal corroding or oxidizing. A primer can also act as a sealer.

The third is the *undercoat*, which builds up the film to form a flexible,

ABOVE A palette of yellow shades adds up to an irresistibly welcoming colour scheme for a baby's nursery.

often called *latex* paint.) As the water evaporates the droplets coalesce to form the paint film. Solvent-based *alkyd* paints have pigment and binder dissolved in a petroleum-based solvent, and take longer to dry than water-based paints. (In the USA these are known as *oil* or *oil-base* paints, though the term 'alkyd' is used for some primers of this kind.) These paints give off a characteristic 'painty' smell as they dry, which many people find unpleasant and to which some are actually allergic. Because of growing awareness of the health risks of inhaling some solvents, the use of these paints is declining in popularity and is already legally restricted in some countries.

Paint also contains a range of other additives to improve its performance. The most notable is one that makes the paint *thixotropic* or non-drip, allowing more paint to be loaded onto the brush and a thicker paint film to be applied; one coat is often sufficient.

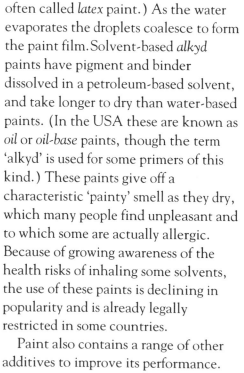

LEFT Paint is not only for walls, ceilings and woodwork; it can also help to enhance the crisp lines of ornamental plasterwork.

BELOW Plain painted walls can be given a personal touch with hand-painted embellishments. Decorators with unsteady hands can use stencils instead.

ABOVE Sponging a second colour over a complementary base coat creates a soft broken-colour effect.

ABOVE Rag-rolling is another broken-colour effect that can look especially attractive when applied in stripes over the base colour.

non-absorbent base of uniform colour close to that of the fourth and final layer, the *top coat*, which gives the actual finish and colour.

On walls, for which water-based paint is generally used, the system consists simply of two or three coats of the same paint unless there is a need for a sealer or primer to cure a fault in the surface such as dustiness, high alkalinity or excessive porosity. The first coat is a *mist* coat of thinned paint. A primer is also used if walls are being painted with solvent-based paints.

On woodwork, the first step is to apply a liquid called *knotting* (shellac) to any knots to prevent resin from bleeding through the paint film. Then comes a wood primer, which may be water-based or solvent-based, followed by an undercoat and then the top coat. To speed up the painting process, paint manufacturers have now perfected combined primer/undercoats, and have also introduced so-called *self-undercoating* gloss paint which just needs a primer.

On metal, a primer is generally needed. A zinc phosphate primer is used for iron or steel, and there are special primers for aluminium. This is then followed by an undercoat and top coat, as for wood. Copper, brass and lead can be painted directly without the need for a primer so long as they are brought to a bright finish first and are thoroughly degreased with white spirit (paint thinner).

Varnishes and wood stains

Varnish is basically paint without the pigment. Most contain polyurethane resins and are solvent-based (like oil paint), although water-based acrylic varnishes are becoming more popular for health and environmental reasons,

CLEANING PAINTING EQUIPMENT

Paint is thinned or diluted if necessary with water or white spirit (paint thinner) according to the paint type. Wash tools and equipment in soapy water if using a water-based paint, and with white spirit or a proprietary brush cleaner for solvent-based (oil) paint. Soak hardened paint in paint remover overnight, then wash out the softened paint with hot soapy water.

ABOVE Coloured varnishes help to enhance the colour of the wood grain without obliterating it completely, as paint does.

ABOVE Varnish is a hardwearing alternative to paint on wood with an attractive grain pattern, and the surface shows marks less readily than paint too.

just as solvent-based paints are losing ground to water-based types. Varnishes are available with a satin/silk or a high-gloss finish, either clear or with the addition of small amounts of colour. These coloured varnishes are intended to enhance the appearance of the wood, or to give it some extra colour without obliterating the wood grain, as paint would do.

Varnish is its own primer and undercoat, although it is best to thin the first coat with about 10 per cent white spirit (paint thinner) for solvent-based types, or water for acrylic types, and to apply it with a lint-free cloth rather than a brush so that it can be rubbed well into the wood grain. When this first coat has dried, it is *keyed* or roughened by rubbing very lightly with fine abrasive paper (sandpaper), dusted off, and a second, full-strength coat brushed on. For surfaces likely to get a lot of wear, it is advisable to key the second coat as before and apply an additional coat.

Wood stains, unlike paint and varnish, are designed to soak into the wood. They may subsequently be sealed

with clear varnish to improve the finish and make the surface more durable. They are available in water-based or solvent-based types in a wide range of colours and wood shades; different colours of the same type can be blended to obtain intermediate shades, and the stain can be thinned with water or white spirit as appropriate to give a paler effect.

Stains are often applied with a brush or a paint pad, but it is often quicker and easier to get even coverage by putting them on with a clean lint-free cloth. Quick work is needed to blend wet edges together, and to avoid overlaps which will leave darker patches as the stain dries. A water-based stain will raise fibres on the surface of the wood, which will spoil the evenness of the colour. The solution is to sand the surface perfectly smooth first and then dampen it with a wet cloth. This will raise the surface fibres. When the wood is dry these fibres are sanded off with extra-fine abrasive paper, ready to receive the application of stain.

ABOVE Varnish can be used to enhance the natural beauty of wood throughout the home, from floors and fire surrounds to storage units and other items of furniture.

SPECIAL PAINT EFFECTS

There is no need to stick to plain colour on painted walls as there is a wide range of special paint effects that will enliven their looks. Some of these effects are purely decorative in their own right; others imitate the appearance of other materials. All can be created with the use of inexpensive tools and materials, and practice and patience will bring highly attractive results.

The special paint effects dealt with here fall into two broad groups: *broken colour* and *imitation*. In the first group a range of different techniques is used to apply a second colour over a different base colour so that the latter still shows through, providing a pleasing two-colour effect. In the second group paint is used to copy the looks of materials such as wood veneers and marble.

For either finish it is essential to prepare the surface of the wall or woodwork thoroughly first (see chart).

Glazes

Most special effects are applied as a tinted glaze which is semi-transparent and allows the underlying base colour to show through. Water-based glazes are made from water-based (latex) paint diluted with water or a proprietary emulsion glaze until the required level of translucency has been achieved. Use coloured paints or tint white paint to the required shade with artists' acrylics. Water-based glazes produce a thinner, more open, coat of colour and they dry extremely quickly, which means they are not suitable for the more complex special paint effects.

Scumble is the main component of solvent-based (oil) glazes and is generally diluted with a mixture of 1 part linseed oil to 2 parts white spirit (paint thinner). However, the proportions can be varied: a higher proportion of scumble will increase the definition of the effect and will retard the drying time; more linseed oil produces a smoother texture; white spirit thins the glaze and speeds up the drying time. Once the glaze has been mixed, pour off a small quantity and add the colour to this, using either eggshell paint or artists' oils. When the correct colour has been mixed, gradually add this to the main quantity of glaze until the required level of transparency is achieved. Solvent-based glazes have a rich, hardwearing

TOOLS AND MATERIALS

Among the tools and materials needed are a stencilling brush (**1**), a dusting brush (**2**), a small paintbrush (**3**), a softening brush (**4**), a stippling brush (**5**), artists' paintbrushes (**6**), cotton or linen rags (**7**), a natural marine sponge (**8**), a rubber rocker for graining (**9**), a large paintbrush (**10**) and a flat-bristle varnishing brush (**11**).

finish and the slower drying times are particularly suited to special effects.

If working over large areas – more than 2 sq m (22 sq ft) – two people will be needed to achieve the best finish: one to apply the glaze and the other to work it. This is the only way to maintain a wet edge and therefore to avoid noticeable joins between one area of colour and the next.

Stencilling

This is slightly different from the other techniques, since the stencil produces a clearly defined shape. It is very simple to do, and can be used to create effects in more than one colour by using different stencils. Ready-cut stencils can be bought, but it is easy to create designs of your own.

CUTTING STENCILS

To cut stencils, tracing paper, some special waxed paper for stencils (available from art stores), a pencil, a pin and a scalpel or sharp utility knife are needed. Trace or draw the pattern and enlarge or reduce it on a photocopier, if necessary. Tape the finished trace to the stencil paper and prick through it to mark the design outline on the stencil paper. Join up the prick marks in pencil. Alternatively, transfer the trace onto the stencil using carbon paper. Cut out the design carefully, leaving sufficient ties to bridge the separate areas of the design. Allow a large margin above and below the design so that the stencil is sufficiently strong. Reinforce any tears or accidental cuts with adhesive tape.

PREPARING SURFACES

The method of preparation varies depending on whether water-based (latex) paints or solvent-based (oil) paints are used for the final effect. Care taken at this early stage will help to ensure a satisfying end result.

Once the preparation is complete, apply the chosen base colour. Use eggshell for a good opaque and non-porous surface if using either a water- or a solvent-based finish and, when dry, rub it down with fine abrasive paper (sandpaper).

Surface	Water-based effect	Solvent-based effect
Bare plaster	Prime with diluted water-based paint	Prime with proprietary primer or PVA adhesive (white glue)
	Apply 1–2 water-based undercoats	Apply 1–2 solvent-based undercoats
Painted plaster	Wash down, repair defects and sand solvent-based finishes	Wash down, repair defects and sand solvent-based finishes
	Apply 1–2 water-based undercoats	Apply 1–2 solvent-based undercoats
Hardboard	Prime with diluted water-based paint	Prime with proprietary primer
	Apply 1–2 water-based undercoats	Apply 1–2 solvent-based undercoats
Bare wood	Apply knotting (shellac) to knots	Apply knotting (shellac) to knots
	Prime with diluted water-based paint	Apply proprietary primer
	Apply 1–2 water-based undercoats	Apply 1–2 solvent-based undercoats
Painted wood	As for Painted plaster	As for Painted plaster
Varnished wood	Strip and prepare as for Bare wood	Strip and prepare as for Bare wood

1 Affix the stencil to the surface with masking tape, aligning it with a true horizontal pencil guideline. Dip the stencilling brush in the paint and remove the excess on some waste paper. Use a pouncing action to apply the paint to minimize the risk of colour seeping under the stencil and marring the masked-off areas.

2 When the paint is touch-dry, release the stencil, wipe off the wet paint and reposition it farther along the wall to create the next section of the pattern.

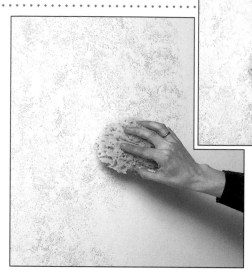

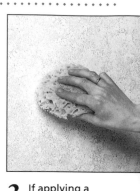

Sponging

This technique involves dabbing irregular patches of paint onto the base coat. Two or more different sponged colours can be applied. Note that a natural marine sponge must be used to create this effect; man-made sponges do not work. Soak it in water first until it swells to its full size, then wring it out ready to start applying the paint.

1 After testing the effect on an offcut of board, dip the sponge in the paint and apply light pressure to leave overlapping splodges of colour.

2 Allow the first application to dry, then go over the surface again and add more colour if necessary to deepen the contrast with the base colour.

3 If applying a different second colour, allow the first colour to dry and then use the same technique to apply the new colour over it.

Rag-rolling

Another simple two-colour effect, rag-rolling involves brushing a diluted second colour over the base coat and then using a rolled-up 'sausage' of cloth to remove some of the second colour before it starts to dry.

The technique works best with a base coat of eggshell paint and a top coat of eggshell paint diluted with white spirit (paint thinner). Use lint-free cotton or linen rags and change them frequently before they become soaked with paint.

1 Allow the base coat to dry thoroughly. Then lightly brush on the second diluted colour in bands across the surface, aiming to leave a random pattern of brushstrokes that allows the base colour to show through.

2 Roll the rag sausage across the surface in a continuous motion. Vary the direction for a random effect and touch in small areas by just dabbing with the cloth. Replace the rag regularly.

Stippling

For an attractive mottled appearance, try stippling; apart from being used as a decorative finish in its own right it can also be used to obliterate brush marks in the base coat beneath other broken-colour effects.

The one item of specialist equipment that is needed to create this effect is a stippling brush.

 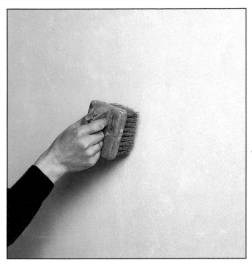 

1 Brush the glaze on over the base coat, applying a generous coat. Do not worry about leaving brush marks; the stippling will obliterate them.

2 Hold the stippling brush with the bristle tips parallel with the surface, and simply hit the paint film. Clean paint from the brush regularly, wiping it with a dry cloth.

Colour washing

This is one of the simplest broken-colour effects. Brush on the glaze and then use a dry softening brush or an ordinary wide paintbrush to create a random pattern of brushstrokes that allow the base coat to show through. A further colour can be added.

1 Brush a liberal coat of the glaze over the base coat. The effect of colour washing is enhanced when there is a good contrast between the two paint colours.

2 Draw the softening brush over the glaze in a series of long random strokes in varying directions. Add a further toning colour if desired when this coat has dried.

Graining

Graining is a technique that aims to imitate the look of natural wood, especially the more exotic and expensive species. Use a solvent-based (oil) eggshell paint for the base coat, and a solvent-based glaze.

1 Brush the glaze onto the wood surface, leaving the brush marks visible along the direction of the intended wood grain effect.

2 Then, after a couple of minutes, draw a dry graining brush or an ordinary paintbrush lightly over the glaze to create the actual grain pattern.

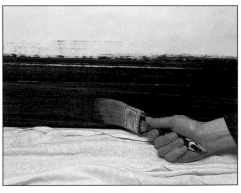

3 Use a rubber rocker (as here), a graining comb or a bristle grainer to produce the individual grain characteristics of the wood you are copying.

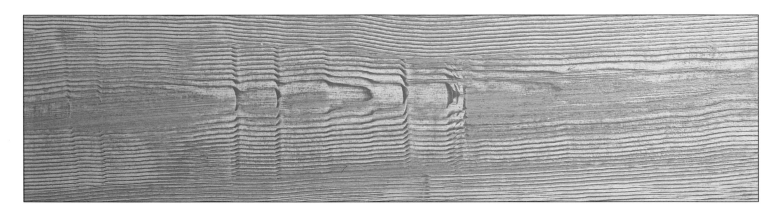

Dragging

Another very simple effect, dragging is created by drawing a dry brush over the glaze in a series of parallel strokes that allow the base colour to show through. Use a normal paintbrush in a width to suit the surface being decorated.

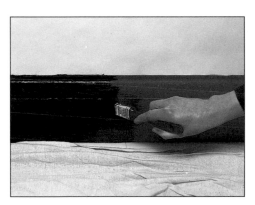

1 Brush a generous coat of glaze over the base coat. Always work parallel to the direction of the grain if applying the effect to wood.

2 Use a dry paintbrush to drag a series of parallel lines in the second colour. Wipe the build-up of paint off the brush at regular intervals with a dry cloth.

Marbling

As its name implies, marbling copies the appearance of marble. It is a relatively difficult technique to master, but the results can be quite spectacular. For a first attempt choose a piece of real marble to copy. For best results work with a solvent-based (oil) glaze, applied over an eggshell base coat. Add the veining details with artists' oils.

1 Either brush out the glaze or apply it with a pad of lint-free cloth. Only a relatively thin coat is needed.

2 Use a dusting brush as here or a stippling brush to stipple the surface of the wet glaze. Add more colour to the glaze mixture, apply selectively to some areas for contrast and stipple the glaze again.

3 Working on the wet glaze, draw in the main areas of veining with an artists' paintbrush and a mixture of glaze and artists' oils. Use different weights of line to create a natural-looking effect.

4 Use the softening brush again to soften the outlines of the veining and to blend it into the background. Wipe the brush regularly to avoid smudges.

VARNISHING SPECIAL PAINT EFFECTS

Some special paint effects, especially graining and marbling, should be sealed with a coat of clear varnish once the effect has dried completely. Use satin varnish rather than gloss unless a particularly polished effect is required. When this has dried, burnish the surface with a soft cloth and add a little wax polish to create a realistic surface sheen, if wished.

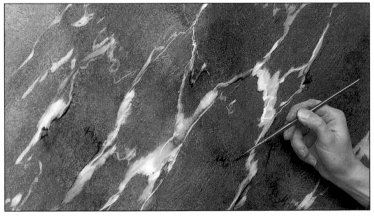

5 Highlight some areas of the veining by adding more colour or a second colour. Soften the effect again, as in step 4.

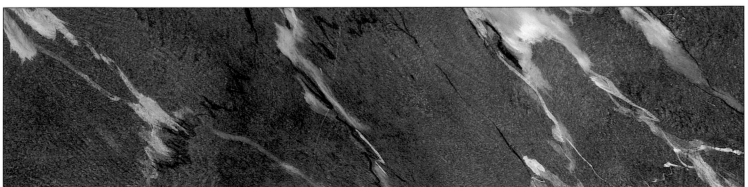

TYPES OF WALL COVERING

Wall coverings fall into two basic groups: those with a printed design or a surface material which is decorative in its own right, and those with a surface texture or embossing which are designed to be painted over once they have been hung.

Printed wallpaper is exactly that – paper with a coloured design printed on it. It may also be embossed along the lines of the design, or may have a distinctive surface texture added during manufacture. Cheaper types may be awkward to hang, tearing easily or stretching so as to make accurate pattern matching difficult. More expensive types, especially hand-printed ones, are better in this respect, but care must still be taken when hanging them to keep paste off the face of the paper. The strongest printed wallpapers are called *duplex papers*, and are made by bonding two layers of paper together during the manufacturing process. Most printed papers can be wiped with a damp cloth if they become stained, but it is wise to check whether this is the case when selecting this type of wall covering. All are easy to strip, making them a good choice if you like to redecorate regularly.

Washable wallpaper is a printed wallpaper which has a thin clear plastic coating applied over the design during manufacture to render it water and stain resistant. As with printed types, the surface may be embossed or textured. Washable wallpapers are also widely available in ready-pasted form. The plastic surface will withstand gentle washing and sponging with a mild detergent, but not prolonged scrubbing or the use of abrasive cleaners. Choose them for rooms where they will be subject to moderate wear, or for steamy conditions such as are

LEFT Stencil borders with the design printed on a clear self-adhesive backing allow the wall covering beneath to show through – the perfect solution for unwilling stencillers.

EMBELLISHING WALLS AND FLOORS

Tougher still are the *foamed vinyl wall coverings*, which have a surface layer aerated with tiny bubbles to produce a slightly cushioned feel. The surface may be heavily textured or embossed to imitate materials such as ceramic tiles and wood grains, and is warm to the touch thanks to the insulating effect of the air bubbles – a fact that makes such a covering a good choice for rooms which are prone to mild condensation. Because of their bulk, they are

found in kitchens and bathrooms. Their main drawback is that they are difficult to remove because the plastic coating stops water penetrating and softening the paste unless it is thoroughly scored first; a steam wallpaper stripper is advisable.

Vinyl wall coverings consist of a plastic film onto which the design is printed, laminated to a paper backing. Again, the surface may also be textured or embossed, or may have a metallic appearance – the so-called *vinyl foils*. The result is a wall covering that is much tougher than a washable type; if properly hung it can be scrubbed to remove stains and marks, although care must be taken not to lift the seams by oversoaking the surface. Vinyl wall coverings are widely available in ready-pasted form, and are extremely easy to strip since the plastic layer can be peeled off dry, leaving the paper backing on the wall. They are the ideal choice for walls that will be scuffed or brushed against – in halls and landings or on staircases, for example – and also for children's rooms, kitchens and bathrooms. They are, however, more expensive than most printed or washable wall coverings, so it is just as well that they can be expected to provide excellent wear.

sometimes sold in shorter rolls than other wall coverings.

Flock wall coverings are either printed papers or vinyls with parts of the design having a raised pile – of fine wool or silk fibres on paper types and of synthetic fibres on vinyls – that closely resembles velvet. Paper types are quite delicate and must be hung with care, but vinyl flocks are extremely tough and hardwearing.

Yet another printed wall covering is made from *foamed polythene* (polyethylene) with no paper backing, and is intended to be hung by pasting the wall and then brushing the covering into position direct from the roll – the material is very light compared to paper-backed types. The surface can be washed, but is relatively fragile and will not withstand repeated scuffing or knocks. The material can be simply dry-stripped from walls and ceilings, like the plastic surface layer of a vinyl wall covering.

An alternative to a printed surface design is a texture. This can be achieved with a paper-backed *fabric* wall covering. The commonest is hessian (burlap), but there are also

materials such as silk, tweed, wool strands, grasscloth and linen, offering a range of softly tinted or boldly coloured wall finishes. Apart from hessian, they are comparatively expensive. They can also be difficult to hang and remove, and so are best used for decorating or highlighting small and relatively well-protected areas such as alcoves. They can be vacuum-cleaned to remove surface dust, and small marks can be washed gently or lifted with special fabric cleaners.

The other kind of textured wall covering is intended for overpainting. These materials are generally known as *relief wall coverings* or 'whites'. The cheapest is *woodchip paper*, also known as oatmeal or ingrain, which has small chips of wood sandwiched at random between a heavy backing paper and a thinner surface layer. The wood chips may be fine or coarse, and the effect after painting is often likened to thinly-spread porridge.

Vinyls are also made as relief wall coverings, with a plain white aerated plastic surface layer that is moulded during manufacture into a range of random or repeating patterns.

LEFT High-relief wall coverings are extremely durable and are ideal for decorating walls below dado (chair) rail level.

Other relief wall coverings are embossed to produce a random or regular surface pattern. Those with a relatively low relief design are generally two-layer duplex papers which are embossed while the adhesive bonding the two layers is still wet; this helps to retain the relief during hanging. Those with more pronounced embossing are made from stronger paper containing cotton fibres rather than wood, and are also embossed wet.

All the relief wall coverings can be painted with water-based (latex) or solvent-based (oil) paints. A steam wallpaper stripper will be needed to remove them.

There is one further type of wall covering: lining (liner) paper. As its name suggests, this is a plain paper used for lining wall surfaces in poor condition or having uneven or zero porosity before a decorative wall covering is hung. It comes in various weights, from 55 g/sq m (360 lb) up to 90 g/sq m (600 lb), and in two grades, white and extra-white. The latter can also be used as an economy wall covering, and is hung in the usual way and then overpainted.

OPPOSITE Self-adhesive borders can be used to add decorative detail to any room. Here they highlight the cornice (crown molding) and form wall panels.

BELOW Borders can be used round door openings, beneath decorative features such as plate rails, and even as an unusual embellishment for panelled doors.

ABOVE Low-relief wallcoverings are the ideal cover-up for less-than-perfect wall surfaces, and are available in a wide range of random and regular designs.

ABOVE A three-dimensional frieze is an unusual way of filling in above a picture rail. The embossed panels are butt-jointed to form a continuous strip.

PUTTING UP FRIEZES AND BORDERS

Friezes and borders are narrow strips of printed paper or vinyl wall covering sold in rolls, and often come in colours and designs that complement wall coverings and fabrics manufactured by the same firm. A frieze is usually applied as a horizontal band running around the room, and can be positioned at ceiling level or next to a picture rail or dado (chair) rail. Borders, on the other hand, are used either to frame features of the room such as a door or window opening, or to create decorative panels on wall or ceiling surfaces – perhaps to frame a group of pictures, for example. They come in a range of widths.

Friezes and borders are available in plain and self-adhesive versions. The former is pasted in the same way as an ordinary wall covering, so this type is ideal for use on walls that have been painted or decorated with a plain printed wallpaper. If a border or frieze is to go over a washable or vinyl wall covering, use a special overlap adhesive or choose a self-adhesive type since ordinary wallpaper paste will not stick to the surface of the covering. Simply cut these to length, then peel off the backing paper bit by bit while positioning the length on the wall.

APPLYING A FRIEZE

1 Decide on the precise position of the frieze or border, then measure the distance from a nearby feature such as a ceiling or door frame.

2 Use a spirit level and pencil to draw true horizontal and vertical guidelines on the wall or ceiling surface at the marked position.

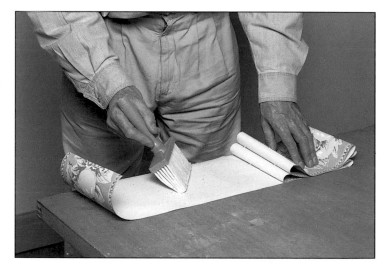

3 Cut the frieze or border to length and carefully apply paste to the length. Fold it up concertina fashion while working along it.

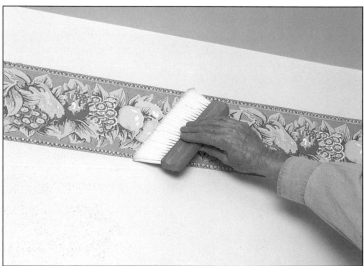

4 Offer the free end of the concertina up to the marked line and brush it into place. It will help to have an assistant when hanging long lengths.

TIP

To gauge the effect a frieze or border will have, and to decide on the best position for it, stick lengths to the wall surface with masking tape before fixing them up permanently.

EMBELLISHING WALLS AND FLOORS

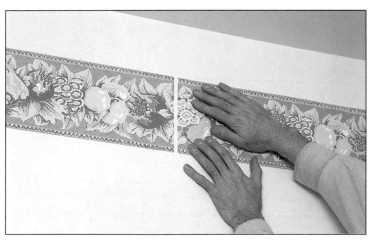

5 Join successive lengths end to end when starting a new roll. If the pattern does not match, overlap the ends so it does and cut through both layers.

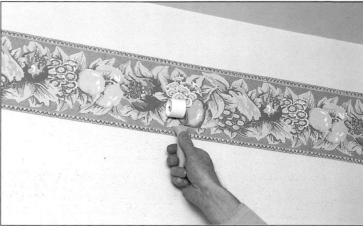

6 Finally, check that all horizontal edges and vertical joints are well bonded to the wall by running over them with a seam roller. Remove excess paste.

APPLYING A BORDER

1 Put up the individual lengths of a border in the same way as a frieze. To form corners, overlap the lengths at right angles and cut through both layers at 45°.

2 Peel away the two waste sections and press the neatly mitred ends back into place. Adjust their positions if necessary to get a perfect joint.

3 The finished corner joint shows how accurate alignment and careful cutting result in a neat joint with the pattern meeting along the mitred cuts.

TYPES OF WALL AND FLOOR TILES

Ceramic tiles provide the most durable of all finishes in the home, whether for walls, floors or worktops, and there has never been a bigger choice of colours, designs, shapes and sizes. The main drawback with tiles is that they are comparatively expensive, so it is important to make the right choice of tiles at the start, and to make sure that they are expertly fixed in place.

Vinyl, lino and cork floor tiles offer an alternative floor finish to ceramics, and offer the same advantages of ease of laying small units combined with a surface finish that is warmer to the touch and also less noisy underfoot than ceramic tiles.

Ceramic tiles for walls

In today's homes, the surfaces that are tiled more often than any other are walls, especially in rooms such as kitchens and bathrooms where a hardwearing, water-resistant and easy-to-clean decorative finish is required. Often the tiling protects only the most vulnerable areas such as splashbacks above wash basins and shower cubicles; but sometimes the whole room is tiled from floor to ceiling.

Tiles used for wall decoration are generally fairly thin, measuring from 4 to 6 mm (³⁄₁₆ to ¹⁄₄ in) thick, although some imported tiles (especially the larger sizes) may be rather thicker than

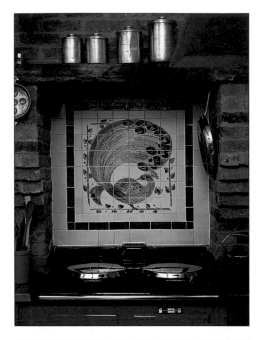

ABOVE One of the most striking tiling effects is the feature panel (**top**), a group of tiles that builds up into a complete picture and looks particularly effective when framed with a border. Tiles set at 45° and interspersed with triangular cut tiles (**above**) can also add interest to the finished design.

LEFT Many tile ranges include a variety of plain and patterned field tiles, teamed up with a complementary border tile, allowing the home decorator complete freedom to decide on the final design.

this. The commonest kinds are square, measuring 108 mm (4¼ in) or 150 mm (6 in) across, but rectangular tiles measuring 200 × 100 mm (8 × 4 in) and 200 × 150 mm (8 × 6 in) are becoming more popular.

Tile designs change with fashions in interior design, and current demand seems to be mainly for large areas of neutral or small-patterned tiles interspersed with individual motif tiles on a matching background. Plain tiles, often with a simple border frame, are also popular, as are tiles which create a frieze effect when laid alongside one another. Some sets of tiles build up into larger designs (known as feature panels), which can look quite striking when surrounded by an area of plain tiling. Some tile ranges still include what are known as *insert tiles* – tiles carrying moulded bathroom accessories

ABOVE Highly glazed tiles can make an unusual and durable surface for counter tops, but the grout lines need scrupulous cleaning to keep them hygienic.

such as soap dishes and toilet roll holders, though these are not as common or as popular as they were.

The surface of ceramic wall tiles is no longer always highly glazed, as it traditionally was. There are now semi-matt finishes, often with a slight surface texture that softens the somewhat harsh glare of a high-gloss surface.

Tile edges have changed over the years too. Once special round-edged tiles were used for the exposed edges of tiled areas, and plain ones with unglazed square edges (known as *field tiles*) elsewhere. Nowadays tiles are either the universal type or the standard square-edged variety. The former have angled edges so that when butted together they leave a gap for the grouting, which fills the spaces between them. The latter, as their name suggests, have square edges and so must be positioned with the aid of spacers.

Both types usually have two adjacent edges glazed so they can be used as perimeter tiles, and sometimes all four edges are glazed.

Tiles for floors and worktops

Although less widely used than wall tiles, ceramic floor tiles are a popular choice for heavy traffic areas such as porches and hallways. They are generally thicker and harder-fired than wall tiles, to enable them to stand up to heavy wear without cracking. Again, a wide range of plain colours, simple textures and more elaborate designs is available. Common sizes are 150 mm (6 in) and 200 mm (8 in) squares and 200 × 100 mm (8 × 4 in) rectangles; hexagons are also available in plain colours, and a popular variation is a plain octagonal tile which is laid with small square coloured or decorated inserts at the intersections.

Quarry tiles are unglazed ceramic floor tiles with a brown, buff or reddish colour, and are a popular choice for hallways, conservatories and country-style kitchens. They are usually laid in a mortar bed, and after the joints have been grouted the tiles must be sealed with boiled linseed oil or a recommended proprietary sealer. Common sizes are 100 mm (4 in) and 150 mm (6 in) square. Special shaped tiles are also available for forming upstands at floor edges.

Terracotta tiles look similar to quarry tiles but are larger, and are fired at lower temperatures and so are more porous. They are sealed in the same way as quarry tiles. Squares, ranging in size between 200 and 400 mm (8 and 16 in), and rectangles are the commonest shapes, but octagons with small square infill tiles are also popular.

Mosaics

Mosaics are just tiny tiles – usually plain in colour, sometimes with a pattern –

BELOW Mosaic tiles are once more regaining the popularity they enjoyed in times past, but laying them is definitely a labour of love.

ABOVE Handmade terracotta tiles exhibit a subtle variety of shade and colour, but need sealing to keep them clean.

RIGHT Ceramic tiles provide a durable and waterproof floor surface for bathrooms. Here square coloured corner inserts set off the dazzling white octagonal tiles.

Modern lino tiles, made from natural materials rather than the plastic resins used in vinyl tiles, offer far better performance than traditional linoleum. They come in a range of bright and subtle colours and interesting patterns, often with pre-cut borders.

All these types generally come in 300 mm (12 in) squares, although larger squares and rectangles are available in some of the more expensive ranges. They are generally sold in packs of nine, covering roughly 1 sq yd (0.84 sq m), although many kinds are often available singly.

ABOVE Cork is the warmest of tiled floor coverings underfoot, and when sealed is good-looking and durable too.

ABOVE The more expensive types of vinyl floor tile offer superb imitations of other materials such as wood, marble and terrazzo finishes.

which are sold made up in sheets on an open-weave cloth backing. These sheets are laid like larger tiles in a bed of adhesive, and all the gaps including those on the surface of the sheet are grouted afterwards. Square mosaics are the most common, but roundels, hexagons and other interlocking shapes are also available. Sheets are usually square and 300 mm (12 in) across, and are often sold in packs of five or ten. The best way of estimating quantities is to work out the area to be covered and to divide that by the coverage figure given on the pack to work out how many packs to buy. Note that wall and floor types are of different thicknesses, as with ordinary ceramic tiles.

Cork, vinyl and lino tiles

Cork tiles come in a small range of colours and textures. Their surface feels warm and relatively soft underfoot, and they also give some worthwhile heat and sound insulation – particularly useful in bathrooms, kitchens, halls and even children's bedrooms. The cheapest types have to be sealed to protect the surface after they have been laid, but the more expensive vinyl-coated floor types can be walked on as soon as they have been stuck down. They need little more than an occasional wash and polish to keep them in good condition. However, even the best cork floor tiles are prone to damage from sharp heels and heavy furniture, for example.

Vinyl tiles come in a very wide range of plain and patterned types, and generally resist wear better than cork, so they can be used on floors subject to fairly heavy wear. However, they are a little less gentle on the feet. Some of the more expensive types give very passable imitations of luxury floor coverings such as marble and terrazzo. Most are made in self-adhesive form and very little maintenance is needed once they have been laid.

DECORATIVE TILE EFFECTS

Tiles are more than just wall covering units; they come in a range of sizes and designs which can also be used creatively in a variety of ways.

The first involves finishing off a part-tiled wall with a band of narrow tiles in a colour or design that complements or contrasts with the main tiled area, to form a decorative border. These tiles are available in lengths that match standard tile widths, and are usually 50–75 mm (2–3 in) wide. They are cut and fixed just like any other tile.

The second method is to incorporate a group of patterned tiles as a feature panel within a larger area of plain tiling. The group may just be contrasting patterned tiles, or may be a multi-tile motif – a group of four, six or more tiles that fit together to form one large design when they are fixed in position. Tile manufacturers offer a range of mass-produced designs you can choose from, or a motif panel can be commissioned from a specialist tile supplier. Plan the motif's position on the wall carefully, and build it in the usual way as tiling progresses.

CREATING A DECORATIVE PANEL

 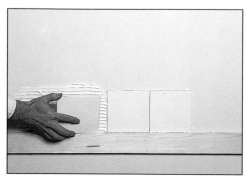

1 Start by making up a tiling gauge to suit the tiles you are working with, and use it to mark the position of the first row of tiles on the wall surface.

2 Put up a support batten (furring strip) if necessary, then spread some tile adhesive on the wall, and place any plain tiles that will be below the decorative panel.

3 Start placing the first tiles that will form the decorative panel. Here the tiles are being laid at an angle of 45°, so half tiles are placed first.

4 Continue adding whole and half tiles to build up the pattern, checking as you work that the edges of the panel are truly horizontal and vertical.

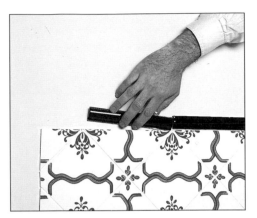

5 Here the panel is being surrounded by slim border tiles. Add whole tiles to the top of the panel first, working from the centre line outwards.

6 At the corners of the panel, fit an over-long horizontal tile and hold another vertically over it so you can mark a 45° cutting line on each tile.

7 Make the 45° cuts on the end of each corner tile, then bed the horizontal tile in place. Check that the cut end is precisely aligned with the panel corner.

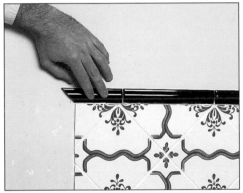

8 Repeat the process at the other end of the horizontal section of the border. Both end pieces should be the same length, as the border is centred.

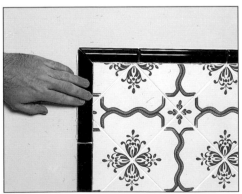

9 Fit the border tiles up each side of the decorative panel, then mark the position of the mitre cut on the last tiles, cut them and fit them in place.

RIGHT The finished panel, neatly centred as a decorative splashback above a washbasin.

TYPES OF FLOOR COVERING

When choosing new floor coverings, remember that there is more to it than simply ordering wall-to-wall carpet throughout, and mistakes can be expensive. Floor coverings have to withstand a great deal of wear and tear in certain areas of the average home, especially if there are children or animals in the family, so choosing what to put where is very important.

There is a wide choice of materials on the market, and laying them is well within the capability of most people. Shopping for floor coverings has never been easier either. All the major do-it-yourself suppliers stock a huge range of materials – plus all the tools and accessories needed to lay them. If they do not stock exactly what is required, there are also specialist flooring and carpet suppliers.

Carpets

Carpets consist of fibre tufts or loops woven or stuck to a durable backing. *Woven* carpets are generally the most expensive. Modern types are made by either the Axminster or the Wilton method, which differ in technical details but both produce a durable product which can be patterned or plain. *Tufted* carpets are made by stitching tufts of fibre into a woven backing, where they are secured by attaching a second backing under the first with adhesive. Some of the less expensive types have a foam underlay bonded directly to the backing; others require a separate underlay.

A wide range of fibre types is used in carpet construction today, including wool, nylon, acrylic, polypropylene and viscose rayon. Fibre blends can improve carpet performance; a mixture of 80 per cent wool and 20 per cent nylon is particularly popular for providing a

combination of warmth, resilience, wear, low flammability and resistance to soiling.

Pile length and density affect the carpet's performance as well as its looks, and most carpets are classified to indicate the sort of wear they can be expected to withstand. The pile can be *cut*, often to different lengths, giving a sculptured effect; *looped* (shag), that is, uncut and left long; *corded*, which means uncut and pulled tight to the backing; or *twisted*, which gives a tufty effect. A dense pile wears better than a

loosely woven one which can be parted to reveal the backing.

Carpet widths are described as *broadloom*, more than 1.8 m (6 ft) wide; or *body* (stair carpet), usually up to 900 mm (3 ft) wide. The former are intended for large areas, the latter for corridors and stairs. Broadloom carpet is available in various imperial and metric widths.

Carpet tiles

These are small squares of carpet of various types, designed to be loose-laid.

BELOW Carpet tiles have a long commercial pedigree, and can be a clever choice in the home too since they can be lifted for cleaning and rotated to even out wear.

LEFT Sheet vinyl can offer excellent imitations of a wide range of other floor coverings, including wood, tiles and even marble or terrazzo.

Cheaper tiles resemble cord and felt carpets, while more expensive ones may have a short or long cut pile. Common sizes are 300, 450, 500 and 600 mm (12, 18, 20 and 24 in) square.

Sheet vinyl flooring

This is a relatively thin material which provides a smooth, hygienic and easy-to-clean floor covering that is widely used in rooms such as kitchens, bathrooms and hallways. It is made from layers of plastic resins, with a clear wear layer protecting the printed design and frequently with an air cushion layer between this and the backing for extra comfort and warmth underfoot. It is fairly flexible and easy to cut for an exact fit; it is generally loose-laid, with double-sided adhesive tape used only at seams and edges.

Sheet linoleum (lino) is also becoming popular again for domestic use, and is available in some stylish designs and colourways with optional contrasting border designs. Lino is more difficult for the amateur to lay,

RIGHT Natural mattings in coir or sisal provide a hardwearing floor covering. Available in a wide range of neutral shades and textures, as well as striped and check designs, they are at home in traditional or modern interiors.

TYPES OF FLOOR COVERING (continued)

however, being heavier, less flexible and harder to cut than sheet vinyl.

Vinyl flooring is available in a wide range of designs, including realistic imitations of ceramic tiles, wood, cork and stone. It is sold by the linear metre (or yard) from rolls 2, 3 or 4 m (6 ft 6 in, 10 ft or 13 ft) wide; the larger width enables seamfree floors to be laid in most medium-sized rooms.

ABOVE Modern sheet linoleum has taken on a new lease of life, offering a range of sophisticated colourways teamed with stylish borders that are perfect for kitchens, utility rooms and hallways.

LEFT Sealed cork flooring offers a unique combination of warmth and resilience underfoot, coupled with an easy-clean surface that looks attractive too.

BELOW Solid wood-strip flooring, shown here in beech, provides a luxury floor covering that looks stunning and will also last a lifetime.

Wood floor coverings

These come in two main forms: as square wood-block panels made up of individual fingers of wood stuck to a cloth or felt backing for ease of handling and laying; or as wood-strip flooring – interlocking planks, often of veneer on a plywood backing. They are laid over the existing floor surface; most are tongued-and-grooved, so only occasional nailing or clipping is required to hold them in place.

Wood-block panels are usually 300 or 450 mm (12 or 18 in) square, while planks are generally 75 or 100 mm (3 or 4 in) wide and come in a range of lengths to allow the end joints to be staggered from one row to the next.

are extremely hardwearing kitchen carpets available, with a specially treated short nylon pile that is easy to keep clean, and also water-resistant bathroom carpets that give a touch of luxury underfoot without turning into a swamp at bathtime.

Leisure areas – living rooms, dining rooms and bedrooms – are commonly carpeted wall to wall. Do not be tempted to skimp on quality in living rooms, which get the most wear and tend to develop distinct traffic routes. However, it is reasonable to choose light-duty types for bedrooms.

Alternatives to carpets depend simply on taste in home decor. Options include sanded and sealed floorboards teamed with scatter rugs, or a parquet perimeter to a fine specimen carpet. Sheet vinyl or cork tiles may also be worth considering for children's rooms.

Room-by-room choices

In principle it is possible to lay any floor covering in any room of a home. However, custom and the practicalities of life tend to divide the home into three broad areas.

Access areas such as halls, landings and stairs need a floor covering that is able to cope with heavy traffic and muddy shoes. Ideal choices for hallways are materials with a water-repellent and easy-clean surface – for example, sheet vinyl, vinyl tiles, a wood-strip or wood-block floor, sanded and sealed floorboards, or glazed ceramic or quarry tiles. For stairs, where safety is paramount, the best material to choose is a heavy-duty carpet with a short pile, which can also be used on landings.

Work areas such as kitchens and bathrooms also need durable floor coverings that are easy to clean and, especially in the case of bathrooms, water-resistant as well. Sheet vinyl is a popular choice for both rooms, but tiles of various types can also provide an excellent surface – sealed cork, with its warm feel underfoot, is particularly suitable in bathrooms. However, if carpet is preferred for these rooms there

BELOW Sanded floorboards can be further enhanced with a delicate stencilled border design. Always seal floorboards with several coats of good quality varnish for a hard-wearing finish.

Adding Features
and Creating Mood

A bare room with its areas of flat and featureless plasterwork and floorboard is a blank canvas which can be embellished in many different ways. Paint effects and wall and floor coverings obviously play their part, but there is also a wide range of other elements which can be added to the room to create personality, mood and atmosphere. Some are purely decorative, but many have a practical purpose as well.

In the purely aesthetic department come fittings such as cornices (crown moldings), which run around the angle between wall and ceiling, decorative mouldings, and fire surrounds; and in the more practical group come wooden mouldings such as dado (chair) rails which prevent furniture from damaging the walls.

A necessary fixture that, if planned and implemented well, always combines the practical with the decorative, is storage – and particularly shelving, for function and display.

Finally, never underestimate the contribution that lighting makes to the 'feel' of your room: creative lighting can even be used to conjure up a variety of moods for different times of the day and different events – for example, transforming a well-lit daytime play or study space into a romantic evening dining area. Few homes make use of the many and varied lighting possibilities developed and explored in many public buildings, yet minor changes to lighting options can bring a home alive.

OPPOSITE
Even in a modern home, without in-built period features, interesting features can be added with relative ease. Fireplace surrounds and mouldings in wood or plaster, and shelving built into an alcove, provide both useful and decorative fixtures to a room.

The walls and ceilings of your rooms can be enhanced in many ways: for example, with decorative wood or plaster mouldings, fire surrounds, wall panelling, replacement doors, new door and window furniture, and curtain (drapery) tracks and poles. Pictures and mirrors provide the finishing touches.

Plaster mouldings

Perhaps the simplest type of ornamental plasterwork is the panel moulding. This is a relatively narrow and shallow decorative strip used, as its name suggests, to outline areas on walls or ceilings which will be treated in a different way to the rest of the room, especially as a way of highlighting pictures, mirrors or alcoves.

Panel mouldings are made in a wide range of profiles, from plain fluted and reeded effects to more elaborate versions such as egg-and-dart, flower-and-husk, Roman vine and Greek key. They are made in standard lengths which vary according to the complexity of the design, and these are simply butt-jointed to make up the panel size required. Corners can be mitred to create square and rectangular panels, or can be formed with matching corner blocks or special re-entrant curves.

Cornices (crown moldings)

Cornices have always been one of the most impressive decorative plaster features. They were originally used externally in classical architecture at

ABOVE Ornamental plasterwork, such as cornices (crown moldings) and corbels supporting delicate arches, add a flourish to any decor, especially in period homes.

LEFT Decorative mouldings are very much in vogue as a means of breaking up large expanses of wall and displaying picture groups. The choice of paint colours is important in balancing the different, defined areas of wall.

LEFT Open fires, whether real or gas-powered, need a fire surround to frame them. Softwood mouldings with marble inserts look particularly effective.

BELOW Even the simplest colour schemes gain a three-dimensional element from the use of wall panelling and mouldings.

the edges of roofs, but were soon also used inside on the perimeter of ceilings. As with panel mouldings, a huge range of profiles is available, from authentic Greek and Roman forms through eighteenth- and nineteenth-century styles, and featuring such classic motifs as acanthus, dentil, swag-and-drop and egg-and-dart. Wall and ceiling projections range from a delicate 32 mm (1¼ in) for single ogee (or cyma) types up to the massive 400 × 100 mm (16 × 4 in) of an ornate Adam-style frieze. Cornices are made in standard lengths, usually 2 or 3 metres or yards. Corners are formed by cutting mitres with a tenon or fine-toothed panel saw.

Plain concave mouldings – known as coving – are also available, made either as a paper-faced moulding with a plaster core, or machined from wood.

Ceiling roses

A ceiling rose is the perfect complement to a room with a cornice

(crown molding) or ceiling panelling. It is a circular or elliptical moulding which can be used with or without a pendant light at its centre. A wide range of patterns is available, from classic designs to plainer modern versions. Sizes start at around 300 mm (12 in) in diameter and range up to a massive 1.5 × 1.2 m (5 × 4 ft) for the largest decorative ovals.

Wooden mouldings

The term 'moulding' is really a misnomer, better applied to decorative plasterwork which is, literally, moulded into shape. Timber mouldings are machined with shaped cutters and routers, to produce a wide range of cross sections.

Most everyday mouldings are machined either from softwood or from

LEFT In high-ceilinged rooms, deeper skirtings (baseboards) and cornices (crown moldings) can help to make the ceiling appear lower. They can be picked out with contrasting shades of paint or matched to the wall colour.

BELOW Panelled doors can be made part of an overall colour scheme by highlighting the panel surrounds to match the other decorative mouldings in the room and to complement furnishing fabrics.

a cheap hardwood. As a general guideline, the larger mouldings – architraves (door and window trims), skirtings (baseboards) and the like – are cut from softwood, while mouldings with smaller and more intricate profiles are made from hardwood. Mouldings can be given a coloured finish, or other woods can be imitated, by staining and varnishing them.

Skirtings (baseboards)

These boards are fitted to plastered walls at ground level to protect the plaster surface from damage by careless feet or furniture – and incidentally to allow floor cleaning implements to be used right up to the floor edge without wetting or marking the walls. Until recently, the fashion was for fairly low, plain skirtings with either a pencil-rounded or splayed-and-rounded cross section; these were usually painted. However, in many new homes there is now a switch back to deeper, more ornate skirtings with traditional profiles, often stained and varnished.

Architraves (trims)

These perform a similar job to skirtings (baseboards), being fitted around flush door and window openings to create a decorative and protective border. They are available in styles to match both plain and ornate skirtings, and are either run down to floor level, with the skirting abutting their outer edges, or rest on a small floor-level plinth block.

Dado (chair) and picture rails

These are horizontal mouldings fixed to wall surfaces, the former about 900 mm (3 ft) from the floor and the latter a short way below ceiling level. They were both popular until the 1930s, and are now making a comeback.

The dado rail was designed to protect the plaster from damage by the backs of chairs, and also provided a natural break in the wall's colour scheme. Traditionally the area below the rail – the whole surface was known as the dado (wainscot) – was panelled or finished in a relief wall covering, while that above it was papered or painted.

The picture rail allowed pictures to be hung – and moved about – at will, and also provided a visual break in rooms with high ceilings.

LEFT Dado (chair) rails allow the use of different but complementary wall coverings above and below the rail. Picture-frame mouldings in a similar style and finish integrate the decorating scheme.

LEFT Cornices (crown moldings) and picture rails do not have to be the shrinking violets in a colour scheme. Here they contrast vividly with the two complementary wall coverings. Picture rails provide an attractive and traditional way of hanging pictures suspended on chains and S-hooks.

BELOW Window dressing adds the finishing touch to any room. Here an attractive festoon blind is suspended from a wooden pole.

BOTTOM Wood panelling below dado (chair) rail level is a durable alternative to wall coverings. The natural divide can be highlighted with attractive stencil borders.

Curtain (drapery) tracks and poles

One last fixture that deserves some attention is the hardware that supports the curtains (drapes). Curtain tracks and poles may be wall- or ceiling-mounted, and can be made of metal, wood or plastic in a range of styles and finishes. The simplest types of curtain track are slim and unobtrusive; more complex versions include cords or motor drives to move the curtains. Ornamental poles are a distinctive feature in their own right.

Wall panelling

This is formed by fixing tongued-and-grooved or overlapping 'shiplap' boards to wall surfaces. It is often used between the skirting (baseboard) and dado (chair) rail, but floor to ceiling panelling is another option. It can also be fixed to ceiling surfaces, and can be painted or stained and varnished, as wished, once installed.

Doors and windows

Replacing room doors is one way of giving a room a dramatic facelift, especially if the existing doors are out of keeping with the look of the room. There is a huge range of panelled and glazed doors now available, and installing one may be as simple as removing the old door and hanging the new door in its place.

New doors deserve new fittings, and again there is a wide range of handles, knobs and latches to choose from, including various metallic finishes, wood, plastic and even glass and ceramics. The same applies to windows. Changing these is a bigger job than replacing a door, but simply fitting new stays and catches can give an old window frame a new lease of life.

PUTTING UP A CORNICE (CROWN MOLDING)

Three types of decorative cornice are commonly used in today's homes. The first is coving, a relative of sheet plasterboard (gypsum board), which consists of a concave hollow-backed plaster core sheathed in a strong paper envelope. It is fixed in place with adhesive. The second is the moulded cornice, made either from traditional fibrous plaster or from modern foamed plastics to imitate the ornate decorative cornices often found in older buildings. This comes in a range of profiles, and plaster types must generally be secured in place with screws because of their weight. Plastic types are stuck in position with adhesive. The third type is a machined wooden trim with a similar profile to plasterboard cornice, and is either nailed direct to the wall framing or to a nailing strip or batten (furring strip) in the angle of the wall and ceiling.

Apart from its decorative appearance in framing the ceiling, a cornice can also help to conceal unsightly cracks which often open up around the ceiling perimeter as the ceiling expands and contracts with changes in temperature and humidity, or the building settles.

FITTING A CORNICE (CROWN MOLDING)

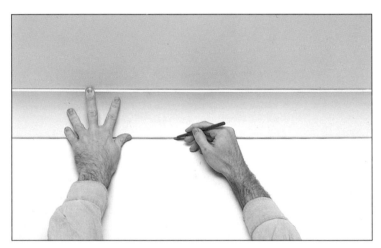

1 Hold a length of cornice squarely in the wall/ceiling angle and draw out two parallel pencil guidelines on the wall and ceiling surfaces.

2 Remove any old wall coverings from between the guidelines by dry-scraping them. Cross-hatch painted or bare plaster to key the surface.

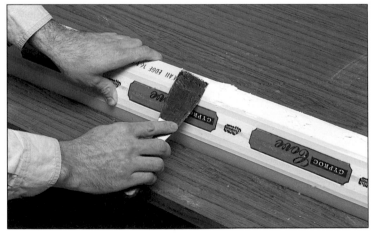

3 Either mix up powder adhesive or use a ready-mixed type. With plasterboard (gypsum board) or plastic types, butter adhesive onto both edges of the rear of the cornice.

4 Press the length into place between the guidelines, supporting it if necessary with partly-driven masonry nails. These are removed once the adhesive has set. Cut any mitres first.

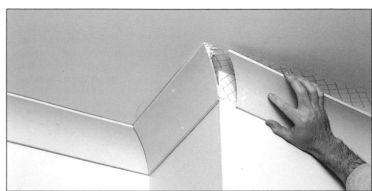

5 Fit the adjacent corner piece next. Here the next section also incorporates an external mitre; measure and cut this carefully before fitting the length.

6 Complete the external corner with a further length of cornice, butting the cut ends closely together and ensuring that the length fits between the lines.

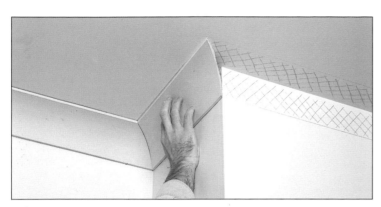

7 Fill any slight gaps at external and internal angles with a little cellulose filler (spackle), applied with a filling knife (putty knife) to leave a crisp, clean joint. Sand the filler smooth once hardened.

8 Before the adhesive sets hard, use a damp sponge to remove any excess from wall and ceiling surfaces and also to smooth over the filled joints.

CUTTING A CORNICE (CROWN MOLDING)

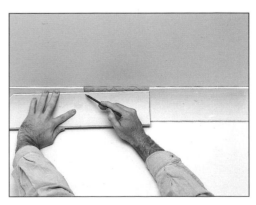

1 Make up a large mitre block big enough to hold the cornice, and use this and a tenon saw to make accurate 45° cuts for internal and external corners.

2 Some cornice manufacturers supply a paper template which enables cutting lines to be marked accurately for internal and external corners.

3 When using cut pieces to complete a wall, mark off the length required directly, square a line across the cornice with a pencil and cut it to length.

PUTTING UP A DADO (CHAIR) RAIL

A dado rail is a flat-backed wooden moulding that runs around the room about one-third of the way up from the floor. Its primary purpose is to protect the wall surfaces from damage caused by furniture – especially chair backs – knocking against them. Once fitted, it can be painted, varnished or stained to complement or contrast with the room's colour scheme. It also serves as a visual break in the surface of the wall, since different treatments can be used above and below the rail – wallpaper above, for example, and wood panelling below. The rail can be nailed to wood-framed walls after using a stud finder to locate the vertical members of the frame. On masonry walls, do not use masonry nails, as the rail may need to be removed in the future; use screws and wall plugs instead.

A picture rail is, as its name implies, used to support pictures. It is fixed to the wall a short distance below the ceiling, and has a curved upper edge designed to accept S-shaped picture hooks, from which the pictures hang on wire, cord or chain. Since large pictures (and also large mirrors) can be heavy, the rail must be securely fixed – with screws rather than nails. As with dado rails, a picture rail can be decorated to complement or contrast with the wall covering. Its presence also allows the ceiling decoration to be carried down to rail level, a useful trick for making a high ceiling appear lower.

1 Start by deciding on the precise height at which to fix the rail, and draw a horizontal line around the room with a spirit level and pencil.

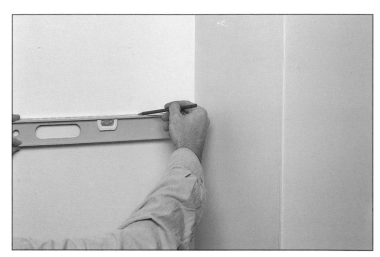

2 Alternatively, use a chalked string line pinned to the wall to mark the horizontal guideline on each wall of the room in turn.

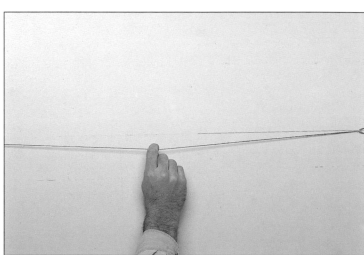

3 Drill clearance and countersink holes in the moulding at roughly 600 mm (2 ft) intervals. Alternatively, counterbore holes for wooden plugs instead.

4 Hold the first length of rail up to the guideline and use a bradawl or similar tool to mark the fixing positions on the wall through the screw holes.

5 On masonry walls, drill holes for wall plugs. On wood-framed walls, use cavity fixings or locate the studs so that nails can go directly into them.

6 Drive the first screw at one end of the length, then the next at the other end before driving intermediate screws. This keeps the rail exactly on line.

MAKING ANGLED JOINS

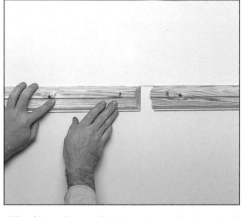

1 If planning to fit a dado (chair) rail down a staircase, draw guidelines parallel with the flight on the staircase wall and mark the two meeting rails.

7 If lengths need joining along the length of a wall, make 45° mitre cuts on the mating ends so that any shrinkage which occurs will not open up a visible gap.

8 Always use butt joints at internal angles. Scribe the rail profile onto the rear face of the length that will go on the second wall.

2 Cut the ends of the two rail sections so that they will form a neat joint line; it should exactly bisect the angle between the two sections.

9 Cut carefully along the marked line with a coping saw, then fit the cut end so it butts tightly against the face of the dado rail on the first wall.

10 Use mitred joints at external corners, cutting at just under 45° so that there is no chance of an ugly gap at the corner.

USING DECORATIVE MOULDINGS

Panel mouldings, made in fibrous plaster, plastic or resin compound, can be used to form a range of decorative panels on wall and ceiling surfaces. These can frame features such as a group of pictures, a large mirror, or simply an area decorated in a different way to bring visual contrast to the wall or ceiling surface. Panels can also be used in conjunction with a dado (chair) rail of a matching moulding, decorating the wall below the rail in the same way as the wall surface within the panels, to help make high walls appear lower than they really are.

Panels can be joined with simple mitred joints at the corners or with matching corner pieces which come in a range of styles, from ornate square corner blocks to elegant re-entrant quadrant (quarter-round) shapes.

It is a good idea to plan the shape, size and effect a panel will have by simply forming its outline on the wall or ceiling surface with masking tape. Reposition the tape as necessary until the proportions look right, then mark up, cut and fit the mouldings.

Other moulded embellishments that can be added with the minimum of effort include corbels, which give arches and mantel shelves some visible if non-structural support, and decorative niches which appear to be recessed into the wall surface.

Moulded plaster or foamed plastic ceiling roses can be bought in styles to match the more decorative cornice (crown molding) styles. These can be used to great effect either on their own or in conjunction with pendant light fittings. The heavier plaster types must be screwed to ceiling joists, but light plaster and plastic ones can simply be stuck in place.

USING PANEL MOULDINGS

1 Once the size, shape and position of the panel are fixed, use a spirit level and pencil to mark the panel outline on the wall surface.

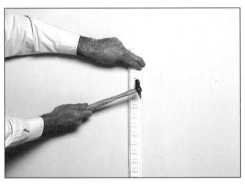

3 Press the moulding into place on the wall, aligning it carefully with the pencil lines. If necessary, part-drive thin pins (tacks) through it for extra support.

5 Square the cutting line across the back of the moulding and saw through it carefully with a fine-toothed tenon saw. Sand the cut end smooth.

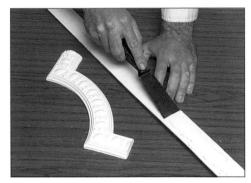

2 Spread the adhesive smoothly onto the back of the moulding with a flexible filling knife (putty knife). Remove excess adhesive along the edges.

4 Before fitting the corner pieces, check that the patterns will match at the joints. Mark the overlap and cut down the moulding if necessary.

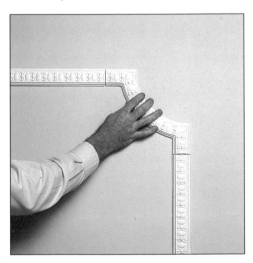

6 Cut and fix all the horizontal and vertical components first, working to the guidelines, then position and align the corner pieces to complete the panel.

ADDING FEATURES AND CREATING MOOD

54

FITTING A NICHE

1 To fit an ornamental niche, spread a generous bed of adhesive all around the perimeter of the flat back, and add one or two blobs in the centre.

2 Press the niche into place on the wall, checking that it is truly vertical with a spirit level. Provide some temporary support if necessary.

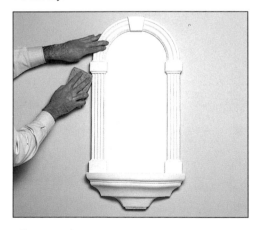

3 Use a damp sponge to remove any adhesive that has been squeezed out around the perimeter of the niche. Do not disturb the niche while doing this.

ABOVE RIGHT The niche installed, with its clever proportions making the recess appear deeper than it really is. Leave the adhesive to harden completely before putting anything on display.

CEILING ROSES

To add a ceiling rose, mark its position carefully, then apply adhesive to its rear face and press it into place. Wipe off excess adhesive. Heavy plaster types should be screwed to ceiling joists for security and the screw holes filled.

CREATING FIRE SURROUNDS

For those who are bored with the minimalist look of a simple hole-in-the-wall fireplace, a traditional fire surround and mantelshelf is just the thing. Complete fire surrounds are made in various types of wood or stone (and sometimes in a combination of the two), but they are relatively expensive and may not be precisely what is wanted. But it is possible to create the ideal effect, and save money into the bargain, by creating a custom-built surround from off-the-shelf planed timber (dressed lumber) and a range of decorative mouldings.

This simple design illustrates the basic principles of creating a tailor-made surround. Start by deciding on the overall height and width, and mark this on the wall around the fireplace opening. Then screw a series of vertical and horizontal support strips to the wall to act as fixing grounds for the various components of the surround.

The surround shown here is made from wood measuring 150 × 25 mm (6 × 1 in) and 50 × 25 mm (2 × 1 in). The mantelshelf and the crosspiece below it are full width, while the vertical side members are cut down in width by the wood's thickness (see step 2). This means that the angled joint between the sides and the crosspiece is not 45°, although it appears so in the pictures (see steps 7 and 8).

The completed surround can be finished with paint, stain or varnish; or it could be given a special paint effect such as marbling or graining.

1 Start by deciding on the precise size and location of the surround. Mark this on the face of the chimney breast (fireplace projection), using a spirit level.

2 Mark the wood thickness on the face of the two uprights. Cut them down in width, using a power saw with a fence or a clamped-on guide.

3 Make up the mantelshelf by nailing lengths of 50 × 25 mm (2 × 1 in) wood to its underside and then pinning on scotia (cove) mouldings as shown.

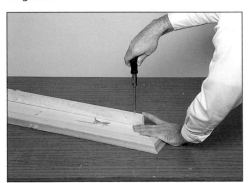

4 Screw a length of 50 × 25 mm (2 × 1 in) wood on edge to the underside of the mantelshelf. Its length is the width of the surround minus twice the width of the wood.

5 **RIGHT** Fix the support strips. The side strip spacing matches the width of the uprights. The cross strip is placed to match the width of the crosspiece.

6 Fix the mantelshelf in place with screws as shown. Check that the cross strip spacing is correct by holding the crosspiece against the two strips.

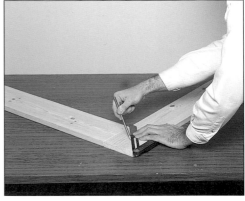

7 Lay an upright and the crosspiece at right angles to each other, and set a sliding bevel to the angle of the corner mitre. Cut the mitres as required.

8 Cut the uprights to length and screw both uprights to the supports. Then fix the crosspiece in place, checking that the mitres are a close fit.

9 Cut a corner block to match the dimensions of the uprights and crosspiece. Nail it in place as shown. Punch in the nail heads.

10 Make up each pedestal by nailing the full-width facing piece to a short length of 50 × 25 mm (2 × 1 in) wood. Support the facing piece with an offcut.

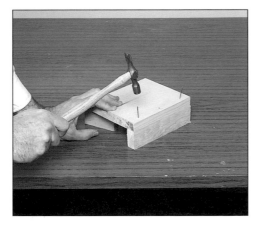

11 Nail the pedestals in place and punch in the nail heads. Complete the surround by nailing two mitred lengths of scotia moulding as shown.

ABOVE The fire surround in position. Add decorative wood mouldings to the uprights, crosspiece and/or corner blocks and plinths, if wished. The surround can be painted or stained and varnished to complement the decor.

INCREASING STORAGE SPACE

Apart from obvious places such as kitchen units (cabinets) and bedroom wardrobes, there are many places in the main rooms of the house where items can be stored. This can be done without spoiling the look of the room. Properly planned storage space can be not only practical and capacious, but positively elegant.

The kitchen

Storage is a serious business here, and what is needed and how it is provided depends on what kind of kitchen it is and how it is used. The fully fitted kitchen is still popular, because it packs the most storage into the least space, although there is now a discernible movement back to farmhouse-style kitchens with freestanding rather than built-in furniture. This is suitable only for people who are either very tidy and well organized or, on the other hand, happy to live in chaos. The style of such kitchens restricts the amount of storage space they can offer at the expense of the look of the room, so for those who have a lot of kitchen utensils and like to keep large stocks of food, a fitted kitchen is a better idea. However, there is one big advantage with freestanding furniture: it can be taken along when moving house.

In deciding what is wanted, analyze storage needs thoroughly. Think about food, cooking utensils and small appliances for a start; all need a place close to cooking and food preparation areas. Move on to items like china, cutlery and glassware; do they need to

BELOW No corner is too small to provide either some useful extra storage space or an attractive display of kitchenware.

LEFT Fitted kitchen storage units (cabinets) offer much more than a home for provisions and pots and pans. Tailor-made units can now store and display everything from wine bottles to the family china.

ABOVE If the fully fitted kitchen does not appeal, a central food preparation area can restore the period kitchen look and provide useful storage space too.

ABOVE Use can be made of every inch of cupboard (closet) space by adding internal shelves and fitting racks on door backs.

ABOVE Pull-out baskets are often more accessible than traditional shelving in kitchen base units (cabinets).

RIGHT Shelf support strips make it easy to put up single shelves or shelving groups wherever they are needed. The shelves are securely gripped along their rear edges and can be easily repositioned.

be in the kitchen at all, or would the dining room be a better place to keep them? Then consider non-culinary items – things like cleaning materials, table linen and so on – and make sure there is enough space for them.

Remember that ceiling-height cupboards (closets) are always a better bet than ones that finish just above head height, even if some small steps or a box are needed to reach them. It is best to use the top shelves for storing seldom-used items.

Always aim to make the best possible use of cupboard space. Fit extra shelves where necessary, use wire baskets for ventilated storage, hang small racks on the backs of cupboard doors and use swing-out carousels to gain access to corner cupboards.

If there is a separate laundry room, it is often easier to split cooking and non-cooking storage needs by moving all home laundry and cleaning equipment out of the kitchen

altogether. Such a room can also act as a useful back porch if it has access to the garden.

The living room

Here storage needs are likely to be firmly leisure-oriented. There has to be room for books, records, tapes, compact discs and videotapes, not to mention display space for ornaments and other treasures. The choice is again between freestanding and built-in furniture, and is a much freer one than in the kitchen

STORAGE IN THE HALLWAY

Simple hooks and an umbrella stand are the bare minimum, but consider having an enclosed cupboard (closet) that is built-in rather than freestanding. It is simple to borrow some porch or hall floor space to create a suitable enclosure. If it is fitted with a door to match others leading to the rest of the house, it will then blend in perfectly. Make sure it is ventilated so that damp clothes can dry.

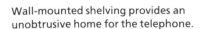

Wall-mounted shelving provides an unobtrusive home for the telephone.

BELOW Alcoves are the perfect site for built-in shelving for books or display and storage cupboards for music cassettes and discs, videos, hi-fi equipment and the like.

While planning living-room storage, pay particular attention to working requirements for power points (receptacles), especially if you have a lot of hi-fi equipment, and for any concealed lighting in the unit.

The dining room

Here storage needs relate mainly to providing places for china, glassware and cutlery – especially any that is kept for special occasions. Think too about storage for table mats, cloths and other table accessories. There may also be a need for somewhere to store small appliances such as toasters, coffee makers and hotplates. Once again, the choice is between built-in storage units and freestanding furniture; this is largely a matter of taste.

The bedrooms

Now take a look at storage requirements upstairs, starting with the bedrooms. Here the main need is for space to store clothes, and this is one area where built-in (and ideally, walk-in) storage is the perfect solution. Space can often be poached between

because here looks are as important as performance.

Built-in furniture can make optimum use of alcoves and other recesses. A more radical option is a complete wall of storage units which could incorporate space for home

entertainment equipment, as well as features such as a drinks cupboard. This also offers the opportunity to include a home office – some desk space, plus somewhere to file all the essential paperwork which every family generates.

USING THE ROOF SPACE

Except in older houses, the roof space is usually cluttered with all the woodwork that makes up a modern trussed-rafter roof and is of little use for storage. However, it is still worth boarding over the area immediately around the access hatch so that luggage, boxes and the like can be put there. If the roof construction permits, however, there is a chance to create almost unlimited storage capacity for everything from hobby materials to the summer's fruit crop. Fit a proper fixed ladder for safe and easy access.

RIGHT A high-level plate rack is a traditional way of storing and showing off the best china. It can be used to display other treasures too.

ADDING FEATURES AND CREATING MOOD

LEFT Built-in furniture is becoming increasingly popular in bedrooms as a way of maximizing the use of precious space.

BELOW A beautifully tiled bathroom is further enhanced with an attractive vanity unit, which can offer valuable storage space for toiletries.

bedrooms by forming a deep partition wall, accessible from one or both rooms; this can actually save money in the long run, as there is no furniture to buy. An alternative if overall upstairs floor space permits is to create a separate dressing room, at least for the master bedroom.

Bedrooms built under the roof slope offer an unparalleled opportunity to make use of the space behind the room walls by creating fully lined eaves cupboards (closets). These are

ABOVE Clothes organizers offer the maximum storage flexibility when space is limited, especially in built-in wardrobes.

WORKSHOP STORAGE

An area where some storage space is certainly needed is the workshop, whether this is a spare room, an area at the back of the garage or a separate building. The basic need is for shelf space, to take everything from cans of paint to garden products, and also some form of tool storage to keep everything in order.

Freestanding utility shelving is the ideal way of providing sturdy and compact garage or workshop storage.

particularly useful for long-term storage of items such as luggage which may be needed only occasionally, as well as providing a home for toys and games in children's rooms.

Do not just restrict bedroom storage to clothes and bedlinen, though. There is no reason why it should not also allow for books, ornaments, or even a small portable television.

The bathroom

Finally, look at the bathroom. Here requirements are likely to be relatively low-key – somewhere to keep toiletries and cleaning materials, for example. It is not a good idea to store towels and the like in a potentially damp and steamy atmosphere. The choice is likely to be between a floor-standing vanity unit and some wall-hung cupboards (cabinets), although if space permits some thought might be given to the growing number of fully fitted bathroom furniture ranges.

Where space is very limited, use might be made of 'hidden' space such as that behind a removable bath panel to store small items such as children's bath toys.

LIGHTING BASICS

Good lighting can play an important role in bringing a home to life, as well as making it easier for the occupants to work and engage in leisure activities. Few homes take advantage of the design possibilities that good lighting can offer, preferring to rely on the traditional central pendant light in each room and the occasional table or standard (standing) lamp.

The following pages show some of the many versatile and attractive lighting effects that can be achieved in different rooms. Before embarking on a radical redesign of a lighting scheme it is important to understand some of the basics of lighting design.

Light is provided by lamps and tubes of various types and wattages. *Wattage* is a measurement of the amount of electricity the lamp consumes. The amount of light each emits is measured in units called *lumens*. Conventional

HOW LAMPS EMIT LIGHT

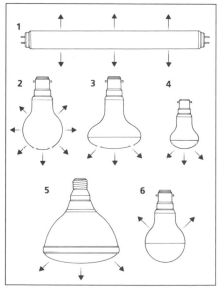

Fluorescent tubes (1) and GLS (general lighting service) lamps (2) emit light in all directions. Silvered reflectors emit it either forwards (3, 4 and 5) or backwards (6).

tungsten-filament lamps – that is, ordinary lightbulbs – are much less efficient at producing light than are fluorescent tubes. For example, a 40-watt lamp emits about 400 lumens, or 10 lumens per watt of power used, while a 40-watt tube emits almost 2000 lumens, or 50 lumens per watt.

The amount of light that is needed depends on the surface area being lit. As a general guide something in the region of 200 lumens per sq m (20 lumens per sq ft) is needed in work areas such as kitchens, half that figure in other living rooms, bathrooms and in access areas such as halls, landings and stairs, and a quarter of the amount – 50 lumens per sq m (5 lumens per sq ft) in bedrooms.

ABOVE Individual spotlights on ceiling- or wall-mounted track provide the maximum flexibility when highlighting particular room features.

There are other factors to take into consideration when working out how much light is needed, such as the colour and reflectivity of the surfaces being lit and whether lighting is direct or indirect, but they are somewhat complex for the lay person to work with. As a rough guide for general background lighting, using filament lighting emitting around 10 lumens per watt, aim to provide about 20 watts per sq m (2 watts per sq ft) of floor area. As an example, a living room measuring 6 × 4 m (20 × 13 ft) would need 6 × 4 × 20 = 480 watts of lighting. For fluorescent tubes giving 50 lumens per watt, you need 4 watts per sq m (0.4 watts per sq ft) – that is, just under 100 watts of lighting for the same room. Regard any additional local task lighting in the room, for reading or studying perhaps, as supplementary to this basic figure.

LEFT Globe lamps have an opaque spherical envelope that is perfect for use with pendant fittings, and look good whether the light is on or off.

ABOVE Downlighters (**left**) and PAR reflectors (**right**) can cast a narrow spotlight beam or create a border floodlit effect, according to the type of lamp fitted.

HOW LIGHT FITTINGS EMIT LIGHT

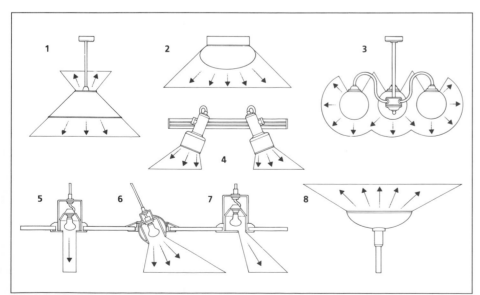

1

2

3

4

5   6   7   8

The type of light fitting or lampshade used affects the way light is distributed. Shown here are a pendant lampshade (**1**), a ceiling-mounted diffuser (**2**), wall lights with diffusers (**3**), spotlights on ceiling-mounted track (**4**), a downlighter (**5**), a recessed eyeball (**6**), a wallwasher (**7**) and an uplighter (**8**).

ABOVE Wall-mounted uplighters are used to wash ceilings with light. When fitted with a crown-silvered lamp, the light source is invisible even with the lamp at eye level.

LIGHTING FOR LIVING AND DINING ROOMS

The key to success with any lighting scheme is to ensure that it meets two criteria: it must give light where it is needed; and the effect it creates should enhance the room's appearance by creating a balanced mixture of light and shadow. The type of light fittings chosen has a major part to play, and so does the positioning of the fittings. The illustration shows how the type and positioning of ceiling lights can create different lighting effects on room walls.

The first basic guideline to observe is to ensure that naked lamps or tubes cannot be seen, by the judicious choice of shades and diffusers. The second is always to provide an acceptable level of background lighting throughout the room, even when additional local lighting is employed, to avoid creating pools of hard, dark shadow. The third is to use lighting to highlight individual features of the room – an attractive alcove, for example, lit by a spotlight, or a run of curtains (drapes) illuminated by perimeter lighting.

In addition, many rooms in the house will probably need local task lighting, for reading, writing, sewing or other work. The kitchen in particular has its own special lighting requirements. Some task lighting requirements can be satisfied by the use of portable plug-in lamps, while others may need more permanent arrangements.

Living rooms are among the most difficult areas to light successfully, because of the many different uses to which the room is put. The aim should be to provide background lighting that can be bright or dim according to the

ADDING FEATURES AND CREATING MOOD

ABOVE Globe lamps with 'jewel' finishes sparkle attractively when lit, and look striking when the lamp is off too.

ABOVE A rise-and-fall fitting provides glare-free light over the dining table, while a freestanding uplighter casts a gentle glow across the ceiling.

RIGHT Recessed eyeball spotlights allow light to be focussed closely on individual features or objects in a room, and can be adjusted as required.

ABOVE For lighting with minimal glare, team an opaque central fitting with strip lights behind pelmets (valances) to light up a cornice (crown molding) and the ceiling surface above.

OPPOSITE Pastel-shaded lamps in opaque lampshades help to create soft background lighting effects that complement the room's colour scheme.

mood of the moment, and then to add separately controllable feature lighting to highlight the room's focal points, and local task lighting where required. The accent is on flexibility. Choosing fittings in keeping with the style of the room will help to ensure that its lighting looks good by day or by night.

Dining rooms have slightly different needs. The main requirement is a table that is well lit without glare, which you can satisfy with a rise-and-fall fitting or carefully targeted downlighters. The background lighting should be subdued, preferably under dimmer control – note that fluorescent lights cannot be easily dimmed. Additional lighting from wall lights or wallwashers can be used to illuminate the serving and carving area, and uplighters for dramatic effect.

WASHING WALLS WITH LIGHT

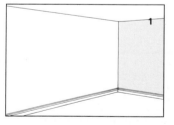

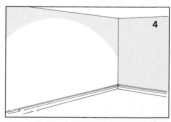

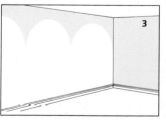

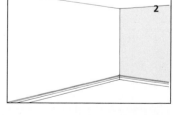

A row of wallwashers of the same wattage create a perfect wash (**1**); decreasing wattages along the row give a graded wash (**2**). A row of downlighters can create a scalloped effect (**3**); a single downlighter casts a parabola (**4**).

LIGHTING FOR KITCHENS AND BATHROOMS

BELOW Kitchens are difficult to light because most tasks take place round the perimeter of the room. Lights above counter tops are the perfect solution.

Kitchens pose special lighting problems mainly owing to the wide use of the fitted kitchen. In the old days most food preparation was done on a central table, so a central light was generally adequate. Now almost every task is carried out close to the perimeter of the room, and a central light – still the standard fitting in many homes – is now useless, condemning the cook to working in his or her own shadow.

What a modern kitchen needs is lighting tailored to provide good illumination at each of the main work stations – the cooker (stove), the sink and the food preparation area. There should also be a reasonable level of general background lighting, plus lighting to illuminate the insides of cupboards (closets). These requirements can only be achieved by separate, flexible and independently controllable light sources.

If the cooker has an extractor hood over it, one containing a downlighter will illuminate the hob (burners) satisfactorily. Otherwise the aim should be to provide ceiling-mounted lights positioned so that they shine directly on the hob without casting a shadow. The same is needed over the sink. Ideally each of these lights or sets of lights should have its own switch so that it can be switched on and off as required. For counter tops below wall storage units, lighting is best provided by striplights fixed beneath the wall units and shielded by baffles to prevent glare. Walk-in cupboards and open display units can be lit by recessed downlighters, and base units can be lit by small interior lights with automatic switches worked by opening the doors. If the kitchen is also used for eating, provide a rise-and-fall fitting or recessed downlighters over the kitchen table so

that the rest of the kitchen lighting can be turned off – not least to hide the cooking debris during the meal.

Bathrooms are much less demanding. The basic requirement is for a modest level of background lighting, provided by a close-mounted central light or some recessed fittings. If the washbasin area is used for shaving or applying

make-up, add a wall strip (fluorescent) light over the basin to provide good, glare-free illumination there. Do not install a fluorescent light if it is to be used for applying make-up. Even the best types give a slightly inaccurate rendering of some colours. There may also be a need for a splashproof recessed light fitting in a shower cubicle.

ABOVE Track lighting is a versatile solution for kitchens and utility rooms, since individual spots can be adjusted to cast light where it is most wanted.

ABOVE In bathrooms, enclosed fittings are a must for safety reasons. A central fitting with an opaque diffuser will cast a soft overall light.

LEFT Recessed downlighters can be used in bathrooms to provide some additional illumination above areas such as vanity units.

LIGHTING IN BEDROOMS

Bedroom lighting requires a combination of restful background lighting and easily controllable local lighting to cover separate activities such as dressing and undressing, applying make-up, reading in bed, or perhaps watching television. Remember that every fitting must look as good from the viewpoint of the bed as from elsewhere in the room.

Background lighting can be provided by wall lights, by table lamps on bedside tables, by recessed downlighters or, very appropriately for bedrooms, with the wall- or ceiling-mounted fittings known as uplighters, which throw light onto the ceiling and completely conceal the lamp when viewed from below. The general light level can be lower than for living rooms, as long as the task lighting does its job. Bright,

glare-free lighting is needed at a dressing table, and good light from above to check clothes. Fluorescent lighting should not be used here, because it falsifies certain colours, so choose ordinary lightbulbs.

Bedside reading lights should be directional so that they illuminate the page adequately but do not disturb a sleeping partner. Lastly, make full use of two-way switching so that lights can be turned on and off without having to get out of bed. Again, choose light fittings to complement the room's decor and colour scheme.

Children's rooms, especially nurseries, have slightly different requirements. Good task lighting is essential for jobs such as changing or dressing a baby, and young children will want a higher overall lighting level

than in an adult's room when playing. They may also need a low-wattage night light for comfort and safety. Finally, older children will want portable task lighting for activities such as hobbies and homework.

The landing and stairwell should not be forgotten. This is one area of the home where good bright lighting is essential; safety is more important than mood here, ensuring that all parts of the staircase are clearly lit without glare. For the best effect, fittings should be positioned so that treads are lit but risers are in shadow. Make sure that any suspended fittings do not impede passage up and down the staircase, and check that recessed fittings are readily accessible – it is irritating to have to get a ladder out to reach a high-level fitting whenever a lamp fails.

ABOVE Recessed downlighters are the ideal light source for children's rooms, providing good illumination of play and storage areas yet remaining safely out of harm's way.

LEFT An opaque shade on a bedside light prevents glare while providing gentle background uplighting and enough downlighting for bedtime reading.

ADDING FEATURES AND CREATING MOOD

RIGHT In bedrooms, light fittings need careful selection because they must look as attractive from the bed as from elsewhere in the room. Globe lamps look good and are free from glare.

BELOW In nurseries, low-energy fluorescent lamps offer the ideal combination of long life and safety, since the lamp envelope is cool to the touch.

ABOVE Halls and stairwells need good illumination for safety reasons. Here recessed downlighters illuminate every tread of the staircase and highlight the hall's features too.

ABOVE A wall-mounted downlighter can also be used to light a staircase, casting the risers into shadow and so making the treads more clearly visible.

SOFT FURNISHINGS IN YOUR HOME

Most items of soft furnishing are expensive to buy ready-made but they can be made just as successfully at home and much more cheaply. Curtains and drapes, cushion covers, bed linen and table linen require the minimum of sewing skills and little equipment beyond a sewing machine and iron.

The choice of fabric plays a major part in setting the style of a room, creating accents of colour to enliven a neutral decor or providing a means of coordinating different elements effectively in a room. Colour is an important consideration when furnishing a room – light shades tend to open it out, while dark and vivid shades tend to enclose it. Many people tend to play safe by choosing neutral or pastel shades which, although easy to live with, can look rather boring and impersonal.

Making soft furnishings at home is the perfect way to experiment with colour and make a visual statement. Most items require a few metres (yards) of fabric at the most. A good point to bear in mind when selecting fabric is that there are no hard-and-fast rules, apart from trying not to mix too many different colours and

patterns in one setting. Most good stores will supply swatches of furnishing fabrics without charge for colour matching at home.

Another consideration is that the chosen fabric should be suitable for the intended purpose – for example, heavyweight cloths will make up into good curtains and cushion covers but will be too stiff and unyielding to make a successful tablecloth or bed valance. A lot of these details are primarily common sense but, when in doubt, be guided by the sales assistant's specialist knowledge.

This section contains information about the types of fabric and curtain heading tapes, tools and equipment required as well as comprehensive instructions showing how to make a variety of soft furnishings from lined curtains to tablemats. When making any of the projects in this section, read through the instructions carefully before starting, especially those which refer to calculating the amount of fabric required. Finally, make sure each stage is understood before starting to cut out the fabric.

OPPOSITE
Soft furnishings in stunning fabric designs can transform a room. Curtains and drapes, tie-backs, piped and frilled scatter cushions and stylish box cushions for benches and window seats are just some of the projects featured in this section.

1   2   3   4

TYPES OF FABRIC

Fabrics are made from different types of fibres which can be used singly or in combinations of two, three or more. The fibres can be natural, such as cotton, wool and linen, or man-made, such as acrylic and acetate. Fabric is formed by weaving, knitting or netting threads made from these fibres. When selecting fabrics for different items of soft furnishing, always choose the appropriate weight and a suitable fibre composition.

Cotton is the most common type of fabric, often with small amounts of synthetic fibres added for strength and to improve the crease-resistance of the finished item. Linen is extremely strong, although expensive and inclined to crease badly; the addition of both cotton for economy and synthetics to help prevent creasing is usual. Both cotton and linen shrink when laundered and this should be taken into account when estimating the amounts required. Some furnishing fabrics are pre-shrunk during manufacture and this point should always be checked when purchasing.

Man-made fibres have different properties, depending on their composition, but the majority resist creases and shrinking. Their most common use for soft furnishings, apart from being added to cotton and linen blends, is for making easy-care nets and sheer curtains (drapes) which are lightweight, launder well and keep their colour through countless washes.

BROCADE
Cotton, cotton/synthetic blend or acetate with a woven self-pattern created by areas of different weaves. Used for making formal curtains and drapes and cushion covers.

CALICO
Inexpensive, medium-weight woven cotton either dyed or printed, also sold unbleached. Used for curtains and blinds (shades), in particular.

CHINTZ
Glazed, medium-weight furnishing cotton, traditionally printed with patterns of roses and other flowers, birds and animals.

DAMASK
Similar to brocade, but with a satin weave giving a flatter finish. Made in cotton, cotton/synthetic blends and linen and used for tablecloths and napkins.

DOWN-PROOF CAMBRIC
Medium-weight plain cotton fabric

10   11   12   13

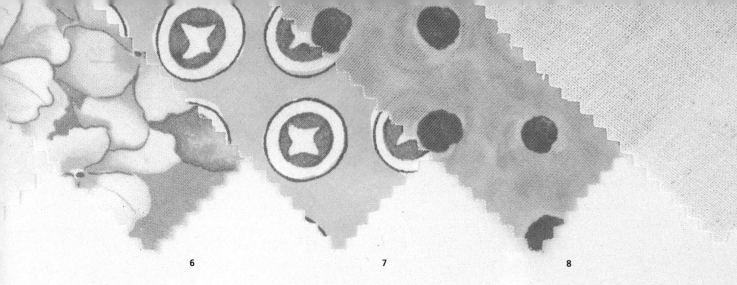

6   7   8   9

Here are just some of the myriad fabrics available for soft furnishings; checked (1), plain (2) and striped (3) in a multitude of different colourways; glazed cotton chintz (4 and 5); sateen in cotton/synthetic mix (6); printed cotton (7 and 8); and calico (9). Other choices include: synthetic weaves (10); brocade (11); velvet (12); jacquard weave (13); linen union (14); damask (15 and 16); silk (17); and synthetic taffeta (18).

specially treated to prevent feathers and down from working their way through the weave. Used for making feather cushion pads and pillows.

GINGHAM
Checked fabric woven from cotton or cotton/polyester blends often used to make soft furnishings for kitchens.

HAND-WOVEN FABRIC
Heavyweight or medium-weight cotton with an irregular, rather rough weave used for curtains, cushion covers and bedspreads.

LACE
An openwork cotton or synthetic fabric, usually with a strong pattern applied to a mesh background, used for curtains, tablecloths and bedspreads.

LAWN
A light, delicate cotton, often with a woven stripe pattern.

LINEN UNION
Hardwearing, heavyweight fabric made from linen with some added cotton suitable for curtains and upholstery. Often printed with floral designs.

MADRAS
Hand-woven pure cotton originating from Madras, India. Usually dyed in brilliant colours, often with a woven pattern of checks, plaids and stripes.

POPLIN
A lightweight or medium-weight cotton either plain or printed.

PVC
Sturdy cotton treated with a wipe-clean plastic coating (polyvinylchloride). Used for kitchen tablecloths.

SATEEN
Cotton or cotton/synthetic fabric with a slight sheen. Curtain lining is usually lightweight cotton sateen.

SHEETING
Extra-wide fabric for making bed linen, usually woven from 50 per cent cotton and 50 per cent polyester or other man-made fibre so it is easy-care.

TICKING
Heavy woven cloth with narrow stripes. Originally used for covering pillows, mattresses and bolsters but today used as a decorative fabric in its own right.

VELVET
Heavy fabric made from cotton or cotton/synthetic blends with a cut pile used for formal curtains and cushion covers. Corduroy (needlecord) is similar, but here the cut pile forms regular ridges down the cloth.

VOILE
Light, semi-transparent cotton or synthetic fabric used for sheer curtains and bed drapes.

14   15   16   17   18

CURTAIN AND DRAPERY HEADINGS

Curtains and drapes can remain drawn across a window at all times, serving either as a purely decorative feature in the room, or a means of disguising a less than desirable outlook. In other rooms, curtains will need to be pulled back during the day to let in light and air and then be drawn across the window at night to provide privacy and keep out the evening chill. Curtains can be made in a variety of fabrics and styles, but they all need some means of attaching them to a pole or rail fixed above the window.

There is a wide range of ready-made heading tapes available in the stores which will help to create a number of different window treatments, giving effects from a narrow ruched band (standard tape) to an intricately pleated border (smocked tape). The tapes are stitched along the top of the fabric, usually with two parallel rows of stitching, then the fabric is gathered or pleated by means of integral cords in the tape. A series of pockets suspends the curtain from rings or hooks attached to the curtain (drapery) track or pole.

The choice of heading tape is largely a matter of personal preference, but keep in mind that the weight of the curtain fabric should be suitable for the style to be created – a very fluid, lightweight cloth, for example, is not suitable for forming cartridge pleats as this requires a more substantial fabric. With all these tapes, follow the manufacturer's instructions to calculate the exact amount of fabric required and how to stitch the tapes in position.

ABOVE An elegant metal pole with ornate finials enhances a curtain with a smart triple pleated heading.

STANDARD TAPE

Suitable for all types of fabric, standard tape produces a narrow, ruched band at the top of the curtain (drape). This type is particularly useful for unlined curtains in the kitchen or bathroom. Between 1½ and 2 times the track width of fabric will be needed.

HEAVYWEIGHT PENCIL PLEAT TAPE

Pencil pleat tapes are probably the most popular type available, especially for floor-length curtains. Use this tape to create narrow, regular pleats on heavy fabrics. Between 2¼ and 2½ times the track width of fabric will be needed with this heading.

RIGHT Make a dramatic feature of floor length curtains by adding contrasting bows and a deep border. The wooden pole blends well with other woodwork features.

OTHER TYPES OF HEADINGS

In addition to other tapes specifically designed for making valances and attaching separate curtain (drapery) linings, one of the most useful types is the lightweight curtain tape for use with net, lace, voile and other semi-transparent fabrics. This type of tape will gather the cloth evenly, but is light enough not to show through sheer fabric and make a heavy distracting line across the curtain top.

Lightweight tapes are made from synthetic materials, so be careful to set the iron at a moderate temperature when giving the curtains a final press before hanging them.

MEDIUM-WEIGHT PENCIL PLEAT TAPE

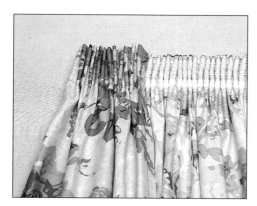

Similar to the heavyweight version, this tape is narrower and ideal for medium-weight printed and woven cottons. Between 2¼ and 2½ times the track width of fabric will be needed.

TRIPLE PLEAT TAPE

This type of tape creates elegant, fanned pinch pleats in groups of three at intervals across the curtain. Double the track width of fabric will be needed, plus special triple pleat hooks to hold the fanned pleats in position when the curtain is hanging.

CARTRIDGE PLEAT TAPE

Cartridge tape creates formal, cylindrical pleats spaced at regular intervals across the curtain. Use a medium-weight or heavyweight fabric to show the pleats to best effect. Double the track width of fabric will be needed.

BOX PLEAT TAPE

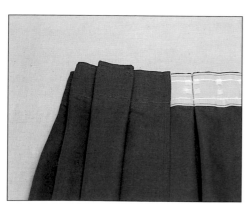

Crisply tailored box pleats are simple to achieve with this tape, which is suitable for curtains, valances and dressing table drapes. About 2½ times the track width of fabric will be needed.

GOBLET TAPE

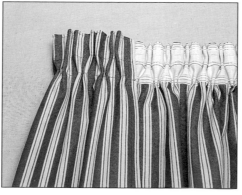

A stylish effect creating neat, goblet-shaped pleats. This tape requires three rows of stitching instead of the usual two rows and about 2½ times the track width in fabric. This tape can also be used to make valances.

SMOCKED TAPE

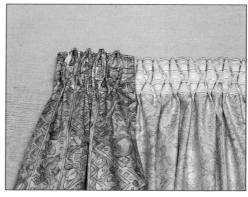

This creates an unusual smocked effect, once strictly the preserve of the professional curtain-maker. This tape requires four rows of stitching instead of the usual two rows and about 2½ times the track width in cloth. This tape can also be used to make valances.

LINED CURTAINS AND DRAPES

Curtains are the largest item of soft furnishing to make and although they may appear difficult, they in fact require only the minimum of sewing skills. The secret of successful curtain-making lies in accurate measuring, estimating and cutting out. Choose one of the curtain heading tapes illustrated on the previous two pages, depending on the required effect and the weight of the fabric, and always consult the manufacturer's instructions when stitching the tape in position.

Lined curtains are suitable for most windows, but for the kitchen and bathroom unlined ones may be preferable, as these are easier to launder. To make unlined curtains, simply omit the lining steps shown below and turn and stitch a narrow double hem along the side edges before attaching the heading tape.

RIGHT Lined curtains and drapes hang well and the lining also acts as a barrier to sunlight, preventing fabric colours from fading.

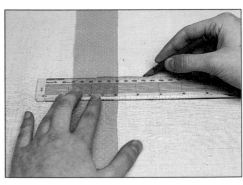

1 Place the lining on the fabric chosen for the curtain (drape) with the right sides together and the lower raw edges aligning. Mark the centre point of the curtain on both the fabric and the lining, using a dressmaker's pencil.

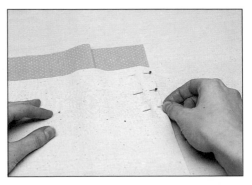

2 With the right sides of the fabric and lining still facing, pin them together along the side edges taking care that the lower edges of both the fabric and lining are still aligned. At the top of the curtain, the lining should be 4 cm (1½ in) shorter than the fabric.

3 Mark the finished length of the curtain and the sewing line for the hem on the lining with a dressmaker's pencil, taking into account the 15 cm (6 in) hem allowance. Stitch along the side edges 1 cm (⅜ in) from the raw edge, stitching from the top of the lining to about 10 cm (4 in) from the hem sewing line.

SOFT FURNISHINGS IN YOUR HOME

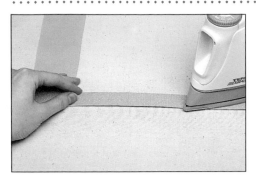

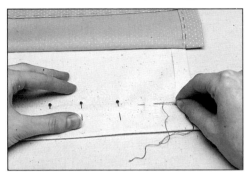

4 Turn to the right side. Press the side edges making sure that the fabric pulls over to the wrong side by 2.5 cm (1 in). Matching the marked points at the top of both fabric and lining, fold 4 cm (1½ in) of fabric over onto the wrong side and press in place.

5 Tucking under the raw edges, pin the heading tape in position just below the top of the fabric. Following the manufacturer's instructions, machine stitch the tape to the curtain, taking care to stitch each long side in the same direction to avoid puckering.

CURTAIN AND DRAPE STYLES

Floor length curtains can add the illusion of height to square windows. Accentuate the effect by holding the curtains back at window sill level with tie-backs.

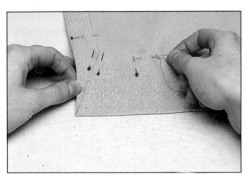

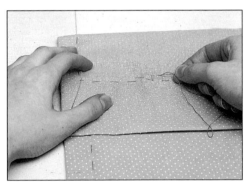

6 Fold over a double 7.5 cm (3 in) hem along the lower edge of the fabric and press in place. If using heavyweight fabric, fold the corners over to form a mitre, trimming away the surplus cloth. Tack (baste) along the hem.

7 Turn up and pin a double hem along the lower edge of the lining so the hem edge will hang about 2 cm (¾ in) above the finished fabric hem. Trim away any surplus lining and tack along the hem.

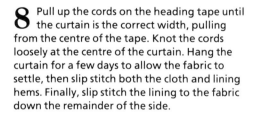

8 Pull up the cords on the heading tape until the curtain is the correct width, pulling from the centre of the tape. Knot the cords loosely at the centre of the curtain. Hang the curtain for a few days to allow the fabric to settle, then slip stitch both the cloth and lining hems. Finally, slip stitch the lining to the fabric down the remainder of the side.

To add width to a narrow window, extend the curtain (drapery) track or pole at each side so that, when pulled back, the curtains do not obscure the window.

CALCULATING FABRIC REQUIREMENTS

To calculate the amount of fabric and lining required, follow these guidelines.

To calculate the *width*, multiply the width of the curtain (drapery) track or pole by the amount of fullness needed for the chosen heading tape (usually between 1½ and 2½ times the width of the window) and allow 3.5 cm (1⅜ in) for each side hem. Divide the curtain width required by the width of the fabric, rounding up as necessary. Allow 3 cm (1¼ in) for each join that is necessary.

To calculate the *length*, measure downwards from the track or pole to the required curtain length, then add on 4 cm (1½ in) to accommodate the heading tape and 15 cm (6 in) for the bottom hem.

To calculate the *total* amount of fabric required, multiply the length by the number of widths needed.

Almost the same amount of *lining* as curtain fabric is needed, with just 5 cm (2 in) less in the width and 4 cm (1½ in) less in the length.

LIGHTWEIGHT CURTAINS AND DRAPES

Lightweight curtains can be made from fine cottons and sheer fabrics, such as net, lace and voile. Shears are used to make curtains for windows where privacy is needed from the outside world, but light is still required to filter through into the room. This type of curtain is often used as a permanent feature, together with heavier, lined curtains which are drawn at night. Lightweight cotton curtains also add a decorative touch to windows and glazed doors and cupboards.

A simple method is shown in the first set of steps, where the curtain is supported with lengths of curtain wire threaded through casings at the top and bottom. The wires are held in place by small hooks attached to the top and bottom of the window or door frame. The other two treatments are less formal and the curtains can be drawn back where permanent privacy is not essential. These styles look best hung from a narrow wooden or brass pole.

The curtain with ribbon bows is softly gathered and is suitable for floor-length curtains made about 1 m (39 in) longer than usual to allow the fabric to settle into graceful folds when it reaches the floor. The eyelet heading requires less fabric as the curtain is not gathered.

CURTAINS AND DRAPES ON WIRES

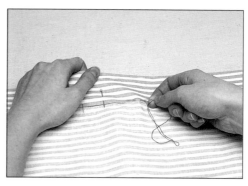

1 Cut out the fabric, allowing 2 or 3 times the window width and 2 cm (¾ in) for each side hem, 6.5 cm (2½ in) for the top hem and 6.5 cm (2½ in) for the bottom one. Turn, pin and machine stitch double 1 cm (⅜ in) side hems. Along the top of the fabric, turn under 1 cm (⅜ in) and press. Turn under a further 5.5 cm (2¼ in), pin and tack (baste) in place. Repeat to make the bottom hem.

2 Measure 3 cm (1¼ in) from the outer fold along the top of the curtain (drape) and mark the point with a pin. Machine stitch along the hem from this point, parallel with the folded edge. Repeat along the bottom hem.

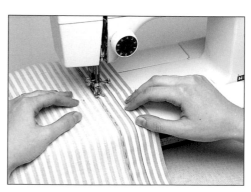

3 Machine stitch 5 mm (¼ in) from the inner fold along the top hem to complete the top casing. Repeat along the bottom hem to make the second casing. (A plain hem instead of a casing can be used at the bottom of the curtain, if wished.)

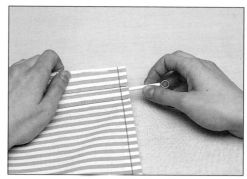

4 Thread a piece of curtain wire through the top casing and another piece through the bottom casing (if using). The screw eyes at either end of the wires are held in place with small hooks screwed into the window frame in the required positions.

ABOVE Lightweight curtains gathered on wires at the top and bottom of the doors enhance a country-style cupboard (closet) as well as hiding its contents.

SOFT FURNISHINGS IN YOUR HOME

EYELET HEADING

1 Cut out the fabric, allowing 2.5 cm (1 in) for each side hem, 6.5 cm (2½ in) for the top hem and 5 cm (2 in) for the bottom one. Turn, pin and machine stitch double side and bottom hems. Along the top of the fabric, turn under 1 cm (⅜ in) and press. Turn under a further 5.5 cm (2¼ in), pin and tack (baste) in place. Machine stitch 5 mm (¼ in) from the inner and outer folds.

2 Mark the positions for the eyelets on the wrong side of the hem approximately 10 cm (4 in) apart using a sharp pencil. Position the hem over a scrap piece of thick cardboard or wood and, following the manufacturer's instructions carefully, use the eyelet tool and a hammer to make a hole in the fabric at one of the pencil marks.

3 Following the manufacturer's instructions, assemble both parts of the eyelet around the hole. Position the other end of the eyelet tool over the top and hit sharply with the hammer. Repeat steps 2 and 3 until all the eyelets are attached. Attach the curtain (drapes) to the pole by looping thick piping cord through the eyelets and over the pole.

BOW HEADING

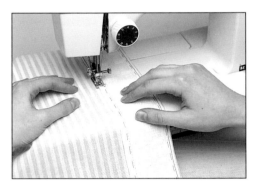

1 Cut out the fabric in the same way as an ordinary unlined curtain (drape), allowing extra on the length if floor-length folds are required. Turn the side and bottom hems in the same way, then attach a suitable heading tape along the top of the curtain.

2 Divide the top of the curtain into 15–20 cm (6–8 in) sections and mark with a pin on the right side. (It may be necessary to adjust the size of the sections slightly to suit the width of the curtain, but make sure that the ribbons will be evenly spaced.)
Cut 2 cm (¾ in) wide satin ribbon into 1 m (39 in) lengths, fold in half and mark the centre with a pin. Stitch a ribbon to the curtain at every marked position. Pull up the cords until the curtains are the correct width, then attach to the pole by tying the ribbons in a reef knot over the pole. Tie the ends into bows and trim.

LEFT The light and airy feel of this bedroom is in part due to the lightweight cotton curtains, held in place with ribbon bows, which allow the sunlight to filter into the room.

WORKING WITH SHEERS

When working with sheers, try to avoid joining fabric widths as this can look unattractive. Instead, make separate curtains or drapes and hang them together on the same wire or curtain pole.

Take care when pressing sheer fabrics as many contain a high proportion of synthetic fibres which melt when in contact with high heat. Test by pressing a spare piece of fabric with the iron set to 'low' or 'synthetics' and then adjust the temperature as required.

PELMETS (VALANCES) AND TIE-BACKS

Fabric-covered pelmets are quick and simple to make with a special PVC material which is self-adhesive on one side and lined with velour on the other. The adhesive is covered with backing paper, which is printed with ready-to-cut pelmet patterns to suit most styles of decoration. Attach the finished pelmet to a batten (furring strip) with the returns secured to the wall above the curtain (drapery) track with angle irons. The batten should be 5 cm (2 in) longer than the curtain track at each side of the window.

Plain shaped tie-backs are made with the help of buckram shapes coated with a special iron-on adhesive. The buckram is available in kit form, pre-cut in several sizes to suit the width of the curtains. Tie-backs are attached to the wall with rings and hooks. Experiment with the position of the hooks, before fixing, to assess the most pleasing effect.

LEFT A fabric-covered pelmet (valance) provides the perfect finishing touch to this window treatment and echoes the shape of the wallpaper border.

PELMET (VALANCE)

1 Measure the batten (furring strip) and the returns. Cut out the PVC pelmet material to this length, taking care to centre the chosen pattern. Cut out the shaped edge of the pelmet material along the correct line for the required shape. Cut out a piece of fabric about 3 cm (1¼ in) larger all around than the pelmet material.

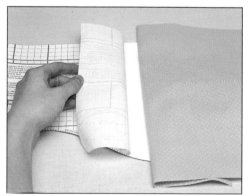

2 Lift the backing paper at the centre of the pelmet material, cut across and peel back a small amount on either side. Matching the centre of the fabric with the centre of the pelmet material, press the fabric onto the exposed adhesive. Keeping the fabric taut, peel away the backing and smooth the fabric onto the adhesive using the palm of the hand.

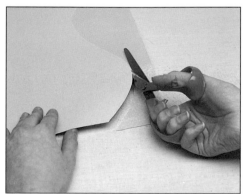

3 Turn the pelmet material so the velour backing is facing upwards. Using a sharp pair of scissors, cut the surplus fabric away around the edge of the pelmet material.

PELMET (VALANCE) STYLES

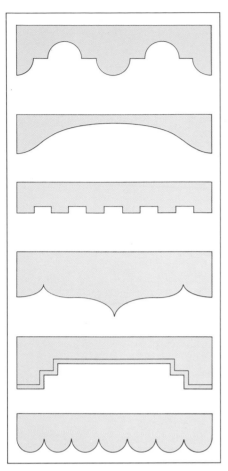

Pelmet styles can be plain or fancy, scalloped or stepped. Choose a style to suit the chosen fabric and the general decor of the room. Always make the shape perfectly symmetrical.

SHAPED TIE-BACK

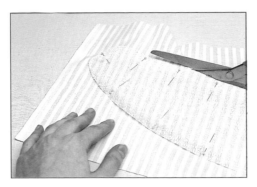

1 To make the back of the tie-back, pin the buckram shape onto the fabric and cut out around the edge of the shape. Lay this on the wrong side of the fabric to make the front and mark a line on the fabric with a dressmaker's pencil 1.5 cm (½ in) outside the buckram shape all around. Cut out the larger front piece.

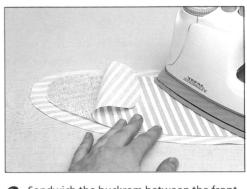

2 Sandwich the buckram between the front and back pieces (wrong sides together) and press with a hot dry iron to secure all the layers together, taking care not to scorch the fabric.

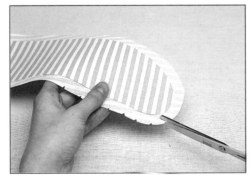

3 Snip into the edge of the surplus fabric all around the tie-back. This will help the fabric to lie neatly without puckering when it is turned over to the wrong side.

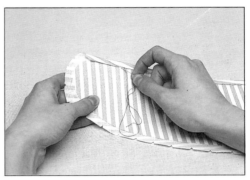

4 Fold the surplus fabric over to the wrong side of the tie-back and turn under the raw snipped edge. Using matching sewing thread, stitch the folded edge neatly in place taking care that the stitches do not go through onto the right side of the tie-back. Stitch a brass ring onto each end of the tie-back.

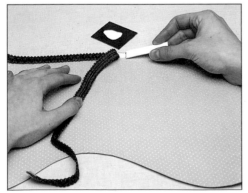

4 For a neat finish, glue a length of braid around the edge of the pelmet using a suitable craft adhesive. Attach strips of touch-and-close fastener to the batten with staples or tacks – use the hooked part only as the velour backing of the pelmet material acts as the looped part of the fastener. Press the finished pelmet in position on the batten.

TIE-BACK VARIATIONS

It is easy to vary the look of plain tie-backs by adding a narrow frill or by binding the edge with a bias strip of contrasting fabric.

A strip of wide, fancy ribbon or braid makes an unusual tie-back – simply apply iron-on interfacing on the wrong side to stiffen the ribbon and cover the back with a strip of lining fabric. Turn the raw edges under, and slip stitch together around the edge.

RIGHT Position tie-backs about two-thirds of the way down a short curtain for maximum effect, but do experiment with the positioning before making the final fixing.

BLINDS AND SHADES

Blinds are becoming a popular alternative window dressing to a pair of curtains (drapes). The two styles described here, although made using very similar techniques, create very different effects – choose the softly ruched Austrian blind for a pretty, feminine window treatment and the smartly pleated Roman blind for a room with a modern decor.

Use a light- or medium-weight fabric to make an Austrian blind – anything from lightweight voile or sheer to standard cotton curtain fabric is fine. Heavy brocades and handwoven cottons are unsuitable as they are much too thick to drape well. A special type of track is needed to hang and mount the blind; known as Austrian blind track, it is now widely available.

Roman blinds, on the other hand, benefit from being made in a reasonably substantial fabric and can be lined to add body to the horizontal pleats and also to retain the warmth of a room. A batten (furring strip) and angle irons will be needed to mount the blind to the top of the window. Use strips of touch-and-close fastener to hold the blind in place on the batten.

ROMAN BLIND (SHADE)

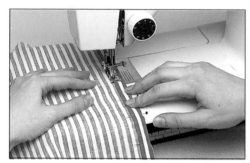

1 Cut out the fabric. Turn, pin and stitch double 1.5 cm (½ in) side hems. Turn, pin and stitch a double 2.5 cm (1 in) hem along the top of the fabric. Press all the hems.

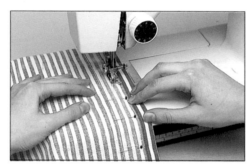

2 Pin and stitch a strip of Roman blind tape close to the side edge, turning under 1 cm (⅜ in) at the top to neaten. Stitch another strip along the remaining edge, then attach further strips at regular intervals across the blind, approximately 25–30 cm (10–12 in) apart.

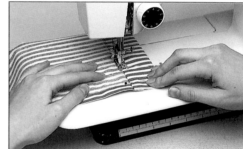

3 At the bottom of the blind, turn over 1 cm (⅜ in) and press, then turn over a further 5 cm (2 in) to enclose the ends of the tape. Pin and stitch the hem close to the inner fold, leaving the sides open.

4 Stitch narrow tucks across the width of the blind to correspond with alternate rows of loops or rings on the tape. Make the first tuck level with the second row of loops or rings from the bottom of the blind. To make the tucks, fold the fabric with the wrong sides facing and stitch 3 mm (⅛ in) from the fold.

LEFT Tailored Roman blinds (shades) are the perfect answer for windows and decors which demand a simple treatment.

AUSTRIAN BLIND (SHADE)

1 Cut out the fabric. Turn, pin, tack (baste) and stitch double 2 cm (¾ in) side hems. Turn, pin, tack and stitch a double 2 cm (¾ in) hem along the bottom of the fabric. Press all the hems.

2 Fold the fabric, right sides together, vertically like a concertina at approximately 60 cm (24 in) evenly spaced intervals and press thoroughly. The resulting folds mark the positions of the vertical tapes.

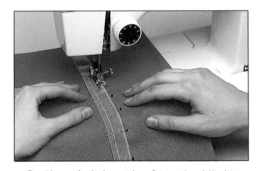

3 Pin and stitch a strip of Austrian blind tape close to one of the side hems, turning under 1 cm (⅜ in) at the bottom to neaten. Stitch another strip along the remaining side hem, then attach further strips vertically at regular intervals across the blind, aligning one edge of the tape with the pressed folds.

4 Turn 2 cm (¾ in) over at the top of the blind and press. Pin the heading tape in position, folding under the raw edges, and stitch in place.

CALCULATING FABRIC REQUIREMENTS

Austrian blind (shade)

To calculate the *length*, measure the window drop and add 11 cm (2¼ in) for hem allowances.

For the *width*, measure the width of the window and multiply by 2 to 2½ depending on the type of heading tape used. Add 8 cm (3 in) for side hems.

For the two types of *tape*, enough heading tape to extend across the width of the fabric is needed, plus extra for turnings. Sufficient strips of Austrian blind tape to position at 60 cm (24 in) intervals across the width of the blind are also needed. Each strip should be the length of the blind plus 1 cm (⅜ in); make sure there is a loop or ring 1 cm (⅜ in) up from the bottom of each strip so they will line up across the blind.

Roman blind (shade)

To calculate the *length*, measure the window drop, add 14 cm (4½ in) for hem allowances and a little extra for the horizontal tucks.

For the *width*, measure the window and add 6 cm (2 in) for side hems.

For the *tape*, sufficient strips of Roman blind tape to position at 25–30 cm (10–12 in) intervals across the width of the blind are needed. Each strip should be the length of the blind plus 1 cm (⅜ in); make sure there is a loop or ring 1 cm (⅜ in) up from the bottom of each strip so they will match across the blind.

TO MOUNT A ROMAN BLIND (SHADE)

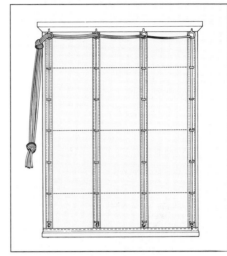

Attach the blind to the top of the batten with touch-and-close fastener. Cut each length of cord twice the length of the blind plus the distance of the right-hand edge. Lay the blind on a flat surface and thread each cord through the loops in the tape. Knot each length securely on the bottom loop and thread the other end through the corresponding screw eyes on the batten, ending with all the cord ends on the right-hand side of the blind. Knot the cords together at the top, cut the ends off level and knot again.

Austrian blinds are mounted in much the same way, with the cords threaded through rings attached to the track.

LEFT Austrian blinds, although made in much the same way as Roman blinds, offer a totally different window treatment – pretty, feminine and very decorative.

SQUARE AND ROUND CUSHION COVERS

Cushions add comfort and a stylish touch to most rooms. Newly covered cushions are a relatively inexpensive way of enlivening a monotone colour scheme as they require little fabric compared to curtains (drapes) or blinds (shades). Simple shapes like squares and circles show off strong colours and patterns to best advantage and both shapes can be decorated with frills or piping or both combined.

Both types of cushion shown on this page have a zip inserted in the back seam – a neater method than making the opening in a side seam. Although a zip is the most convenient method of fastening a cushion cover, making it easy to remove for laundering, the opening may be closed with a row of slip stitches which need to be replaced whenever the cover is removed.

SQUARE CUSHION COVER

1 Measure the cushion pad, adding 1.5 cm (½ in) all around for ease, plus 1.5 cm (½ in) for seam allowances. Do not forget to allow an extra 3 cm (1 in) for the centre back seam. Cut out the front and two back pieces. Pin and stitch the centre back seam 1.5 cm (½ in) from the raw edges, making sure to leave an opening to accommodate the zip fastener. Press the seam open.

BELOW Frills and piping in matching or contrasting fabric add a special touch to round and square cushion covers.

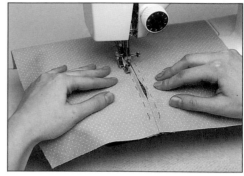

2 Pin and tack (baste) the zip in position along the opening, as shown, allowing the fabric to meet centrally over the zip teeth. Machine stitch the zip in place using a zip foot on the machine.

3 Press the seam allowances around the zip. Open the zip, making sure the fabric does not catch in the teeth and the ends are stitched securely. With the zip still open, place the front and back pieces together so that the right sides are facing.

4 Pin and machine stitch twice around the edge about 1.5 cm (½ in) from the raw edge. Clip the surplus fabric away close to the stitching at the corners to reduce the bulk. Press the seams and turn the cover to the right side through the zipped opening. Press the seams, insert the cushion pad and close the zip.

FRILLS

To make a frill, a piece of fabric is needed which is twice the depth of the finished frill plus 3 cm (1¼ in), and between 1½ and 2 times the outside measurement of the cover. You may need to join several strips together to achieve the right length.

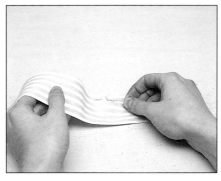

1 Join the ends of the strips together with a flat seam. Fold the strip in half lengthways with the wrong sides facing. Make one or two rows of running stitches along the raw edges of the strip, taking the stitches through both layers and leaving a long end of thread at one end of each row.

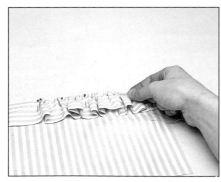

2 Gather the frill by pulling up the long threads until the frill is the right size to fit around the cushion front. Wind the long threads around a pin to secure them and even out the gather with the fingers.
  To add a frill to either a square or round cushion, align the raw edge of the frill with the raw edge of the front cover, right sides together. Tack and sew the frill in place, then continue making up the cover in the usual way.

RIGHT Choose sumptuous fabrics for cushion covers to complement curtains and wall coverings for a harmonious decorating scheme.

ROUND CUSHION COVER

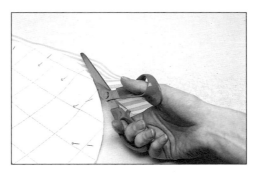

1 Measure the diameter of the cushion pad and add 1.5 cm (½ in) all around for ease, plus 1.5 cm (½ in) for seam allowances. Make a paper pattern to this size using dressmaker's pattern paper. Pin onto the fabric and cut out one piece for the front of the cover.

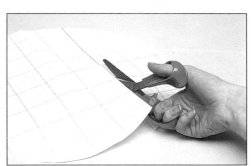

2 Rule a line across the paper pattern to mark the position of the back seam. The line should measure approximately 12.5 cm (5 in) longer than the zip. Cut the paper pattern in two along this line.

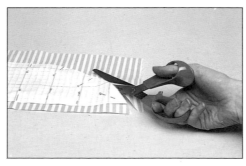

3 Pin both pattern pieces onto the fabric and cut out, remembering to allow an extra 1.5 cm (½ in) for the seam allowance on the straight edge of each piece.

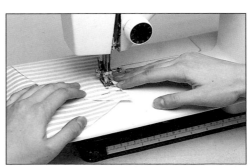

4 Pin and stitch the back seam, making sure to leave an opening which is long enough to accommodate the zip fastener. Finish off the cover in the same way as the square cover.

BOX AND BOLSTER CUSHIONS

Box cushion covers are often made to fit a particular chair or window seat as they can accommodate a thick cushion pad or piece of foam block. The covers should look neatly tailored and are best made in a crisp, cotton furnishing fabric. The seams can be enhanced with piping made from matching or contrasting fabric – plain piping looks particularly effective with patterned cushion fabric. Always pre-shrink cotton piping cord by washing it in hot water before use.

Circular bolster cushions look attractive on most types of furniture and make a good visual contrast against the more usual rectangular cushions. This shape of cushion works particularly well with striped, check and tartan cloth, especially when a contrasting tassel, ribbon bow or pompon is used as a trim.

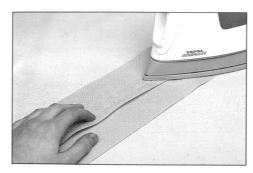

1 Cut out the fabric. Cut the back gusset in half lengthways and place together with the right sides facing. Pin and stitch the seam 1.5 cm (½ in) from the raw edges, leaving an opening for the zip. Press the seam open.

2 Pin and tack the zip in position along the opening, as shown, allowing the fabric to meet centrally over the zip teeth. Stitch the zip in place using a zip foot on the machine.

3 With the right sides facing, join the four gusset pieces together along the short ends, taking a 1.5 cm (½ in) seam allowance and leaving 1.5 cm (½ in) unstitched at each end of the seams. Press the seams open.

4 With the right sides facing, pin and stitch the top edge of one gusset section to one edge of the top cover piece, taking a 1.5 cm (½ in) seam allowance. At the gusset seam, leave the needle in the fabric, raise the machine foot and pivot the fabric so the next section of gusset aligns with the next side of the top cover piece. Continue pinning and stitching each section around the top in this way. Open the zip, then repeat the procedure to attach the bottom cover piece to the remaining side of the gusset. Trim away the surplus cloth at the corners and then turn the cover right side out through the zip opening.

FRENCH SEAMS

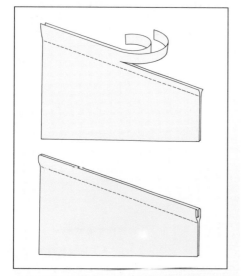

A French seam encloses the raw edges of fabric and prevents them fraying. It is worked in two stages: first stitch with the pieces wrong sides facing (**TOP**). Trim down the raw edges close to the first row of stitching. Then stitch with the right sides facing (**ABOVE**).

BELOW A box cushion adds comfort and style to an attractive bench. The seams have been piped in a contrasting fabric to accentuate the boxy shape.

BOLSTER CUSHION

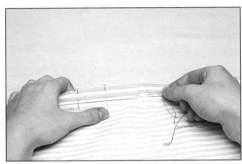

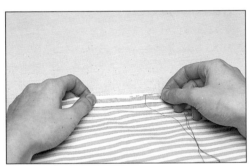

CALCULATING FABRIC REQUIREMENTS

Box cushion

Measure the length and width of the top of the pad and add 1.5 cm (½ in) all around for seam allowances. Two pieces of fabric this size are needed, one for the top and one for the bottom of the cover. The gusset is made from four pieces of fabric joined together. Measure the depth and width of the pad and add 1.5 cm (½ in) all around for seam allowances. Cut out three pieces of fabric to this size. Add an extra 3 cm (1 in) to the depth of the fourth piece for the zip seam in the back gusset.

Bolster cushion

To calculate the *length*, measure the bolster from the centre point of one end, along the length and around to the centre point of the opposite end, adding a total of 6 cm (2 in) for hem allowances.

To calculate the *width*, measure the circumference of the pad and add 3 cm (1 in) for seam allowances.

1 Cut out the fabric. Pin and stitch the length of the bolster cover with a French seam (see illustrations). Turn the resulting tube right side out and press the seam.

2 Turn under a double 1.5 cm (½ in) hem at each end of the tube. Pin and tack (baste) the hem in place using a contrasting coloured thread so the stitches are easy to detect.

3 Machine stitch along the hems, keeping the stitching close to the inner folds. Remove the tacking stitches and press thoroughly.

ABOVE Gathered bolsters contrast well with the more usual rectangular cushion shapes.

4 Using double thread run a row of gathering stitches along each end of the tube, close to the outer fold of the hem and leaving a long thread end. Insert the bolster pad in the tube, then tighten the gathering threads to close the cover. Secure the thread ends, then cover the small hole left at each end by attaching a furnishing tassel, ribbon bow or a covered button.

PIPING

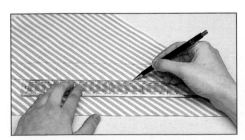

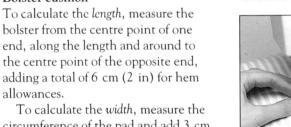

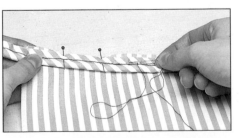

1 Fold a piece of fabric in half diagonally and press the fold. Open out the fabric and using a ruler and pencil, mark out strips parallel to the fold about 4–5 cm (1½–2 in) apart, depending on the thickness of the piping cord. Cut out the strips.

2 Join the strips together with a flat seam to make the required length. Place the piping cord along the centre of the strip, fold it over with wrong sides facing and pin together. Tack (baste) and stitch close to the cord.

3 Lay the covered cord on the right side of the fabric with raw edges aligning and tack in place. Cover with a second piece of fabric, right side downwards and raw edges matching. Stitch the layers together along the seamline using a zip foot on the machine. Remove the tacking stitches.

TABLECLOTHS

Both square and round tablecloths are quick to make. For practical uses choose a washable fabric, either plain or patterned, in a shade which matches or coordinates with the general colour scheme of the room as well as any favourite tableware.

Cotton and synthetic blends are easy to sew, require practically no ironing and so make a good choice for everyday tablecloths in the kitchen or dining room. Plain, heavy cotton and linen look better for more formal occasions, but they require more hard work to keep them looking good over the years. Always treat stains on table linen immediately and launder as soon afterwards as possible.

SQUARE TABLECLOTH

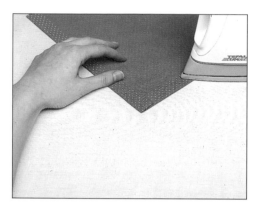

1 Measure the sides of the table top, adding twice the required drop from the edge of the table and 3 cm (1 in) all around for hem allowances. Cut out the fabric. Turn and press a double 1.5 cm (½ in) hem around the sides.

BELOW Choose a pretty printed fabric to make a covering for a rectangular kitchen table.

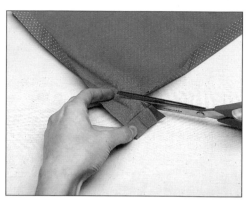

2 Unfold both hems and cut across each corner diagonally, as shown, within 5 mm (¼ in) of the corner point at the inner fold.

3 Pin the diagonal edges together, with the right sides facing, and stitch a narrow seam 5 mm (¼ in) from the raw edge. Stitch from the inner corner point and make the seam 1.5 cm (½ in) long. Press each seam and turn the corners out to the right side.

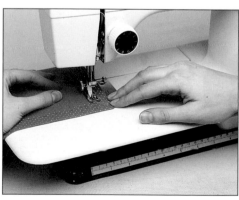

4 Re-fold the double hem along the pressed lines. The diagonal seams at each corner make a neat mitre. Pin, tack (baste) and stitch around the edge of the tablecloth, close to the inner fold. Press the hem.

RIGHT Cover a round occasional table with a floor-length plain undercloth, then top it with a small square cloth made of coordinating fabric.

JOINING FABRIC

When joining fabric to make either a square or round tablecloth, avoid making a seam down the centre as this can look rather unsightly. Instead, cut out two pieces of fabric to the correct width and use one as the central panel. Cut the second piece in half lengthways and join to either side of the panel, matching the pattern if necessary. Use an ordinary flat seam and neaten the raw edges.

ROUND TABLECLOTH

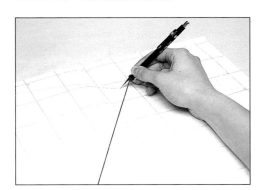

1 Measure the diameter of the table top and add twice the depth of the drop plus 3 cm (1 in) for hem allowances. Make a pattern from dressmaker's pattern paper using a pencil tied to a piece of string measuring half your final measurement. Hold one end of the string down on the paper, pull the string taut and draw a quarter circle on the paper with the pencil. Cut out the pattern.

2 Fold the fabric into four and pin on the quarter circle pattern, aligning the folded edges of the fabric with the straight edges of the paper. Cut out using sharp scissors.

3 Stitch around the outside of the fabric 1.5 cm (½ in) from the raw edge. This line of stitching marks the hem edge. Press the edge over onto the wrong side of the fabric along the stitched line without stretching the fabric.

4 Carefully turn under the raw edge to make a double hem, then pin and tack (baste) the hem in place. Stitch around the edge of the tablecloth close to the inner fold of the hem. Press the hem well.

TABLEMATS AND NAPKINS

Tablemats and napkins make the perfect table setting for an informal meal. They are simple to make and can be a good way of using offcuts and remnants of fabric.

Tablemats can be made from plain or patterned fabric and are most effective when machine quilted with a layer of wadding (batting) sandwiched between the top and bottom pieces of fabric. The layers help to protect the table surface beneath the plates. Bind the edges with matching or contrasting fabric or ready-made bias binding. Alternatively, choose ready-quilted fabric and follow the instructions for binding given here to finish the edges.

Napkins are simply a hemmed piece of fabric, usually square and made in a cloth which coordinates with the tablemats or a tablecloth. Give some thought to the practical purpose of napkins and always make them from fabric which is washable. Polyester and cotton blends are a popular choice for informal napkins, but nothing beats the look of pure linen for a formal occasion.

TABLEMAT

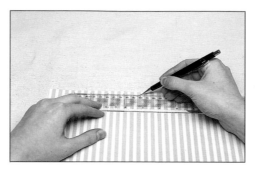

1 Decide on the size of the tablemat and cut out two pieces of fabric. Along the short edge of one piece, mark evenly spaced points 2.5 cm (1 in) apart using a ruler and a sharp pencil. Join the points to make lines running across the fabric.

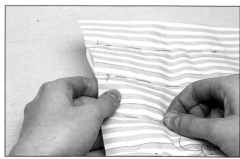

2 Cut a piece of wadding (batting) to the same size as the fabric and sandwich it between the two fabric pieces, with the wrong sides together and the marked piece on top. Pin together carefully, then work rows of tacking (basting) between alternate pencil lines.

3 Lengthen the stitch on the sewing machine slightly, then work parallel rows of machine stitching over the pencil lines using a matching or contrasting thread. Round off the corners by drawing around a cup or small plate, then trim away the surplus fabric.

4 Cut out and join the bias strips until the strip of binding is long enough to go around the edge of the tablemat. Fold the strip so that the raw edges meet in the middle and press. Open out one folded edge of the binding and pin it around the tablemat with the right sides facing and raw edges aligning. Neatly fold back the raw edges where the binding meets. Stitch along the crease of the binding.

SIZES AND FABRIC REQUIREMENTS

Tablemats

To decide on a suitable size for tablemats, first arrange a place setting with two sizes of plate plus cutlery (flatware) and measure the area these cover. The side plate and glass can be placed on the table at the edge of the mat, if preferred.

Traditionally, rectangular tablemats measure approximately 20 × 30 cm (8 × 12 in), but they can be larger – up to 30 × 45 cm (12 × 18 in). Having decided on the finished size of the tablemats, allow at least 5 cm (2 in)

extra all around for working the quilting. Always trim the surplus fabric away after completing the machine quilting but before beginning to bind the edges.

Napkins

Napkins are usually square and vary in size from small napkins of 30 cm (12 in) square for tea or coffee parties to large ones measuring 60 cm (24 in) for formal occasions. However, a good all-purpose size for napkins is 40 cm (16 in) square.

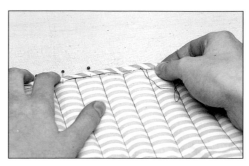

5 Fold over the binding to the wrong side of the tablemat. Pin and stitch the binding in place by hand as shown. Turn the tablemat to the right side and strengthen the edge by working one row of machine stitching around the edge close to the inside fold of the binding.

RIGHT For a heavily-quilted tablemat, work two sets of parallel quilting lines across the fabric to make diamond shapes, then bind the edges with plain fabric.

NAPKIN

Cut out the fabric to the required size. Fold and press a double 5 mm (¼ in) hem all around the edge, taking care to fold the corners over neatly. Pin, tack (baste) and stitch the hem close to the inner fold.

BELOW Make a feature of a linen napkin by adding a bow of narrow ribbon and dainty fresh flowerhead.

BIAS STRIPS

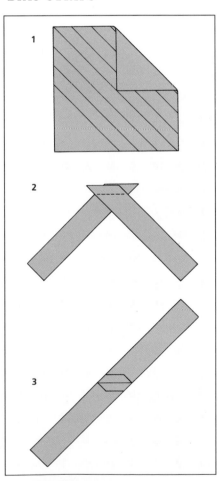

To make bias strips, mark out parallel lines the required distance apart on the cross of the fabric using a ruler and pencil (**1**). Cut out along the lines, then join the strips together with narrow seams until you have the required length (**2**). Press the seams open (**3**).

BED LINEN

Be imaginative in choosing colour schemes and pattern combinations for bed linen. A matching duvet cover and valance looks stylish, particularly when the fabric coordinates with the curtains or drapes and other bedroom furnishings.

The duvet cover is simply a large bag made from two pieces of fabric joined together around the four sides, with an opening left in the bottom edge to allow the duvet to be inserted. Close the opening with either touch-and-close fastener or press stud tape. The valance fits over the bed base, underneath the mattress, and has a frill around three sides reaching right down to floor level.

RIGHT A matching gathered valance finishes off this arrangement perfectly. Lace edging around the pillows and duvet cover adds a feminine touch.

DUVET COVER

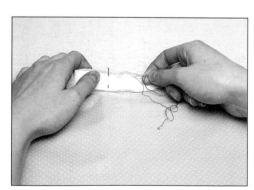
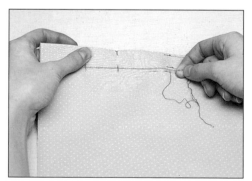

1 Measure the length of the duvet, usually 200 cm (78 in), and add 7 cm (2¾ in) for hem and seam allowances. Measure the width and add 4 cm (1½ in) for seam allowances. Cut out two pieces of fabric. Turn and stitch a double 2.5 cm (1 in) hem along the bottom of each piece. Cut a length of touch-and-close fastener 3 cm (1¼ in) longer than the desired opening, separate the strips and pin one to the right side of the hem on each piece. Machine stitch in place around the edge of each strip.

2 Place the two fabric pieces with right sides together so the fastener strips close. Tack (baste) along the bottom hem from 3 cm (1¼ in) inside the strip of fastener and up to each corner.

3 Machine stitch through both layers at right angles to the hem 3 cm (1¼ in) inside the fastener strip to enclose the raw edges. Pivot the fabric and continue stitching along the tacked line to the edge of the fabric. Repeat at the other corner.

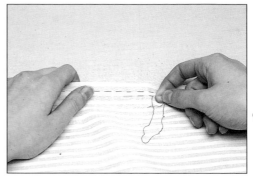

1 Measure the mattress top and add 3.5 cm (1½ in) to the length and 3 cm (1 in) to the width. Cut out one piece of fabric to this size for the panel. Round off the two bottom corners of the panel by drawing around a plate and cutting around the curves.

2 For the frill, sufficient pieces of fabric wide enough to reach from the top of the bed base to the floor, plus 6.5 cm (2½ in), are needed to make a long strip four times the mattress length plus twice the mattress width. Join the strips with French seams (see Duvet Cover, step 4) and press. Turn a double 2.5 cm (1 in) hem along the lower edge of the frill. Pin, tack (baste) and stitch as shown.

3 Divide the frill into six equal sections and mark with pins along the top edge. Work two rows of gathering stitches between the pins, leaving long thread ends.

CHOOSING FABRIC FOR BED LINEN

The best choice for bed linen is specially woven sheeting either in pure cotton or a polyester and cotton blend. Although pure cotton is cooler in summer, synthetic blends do have the advantage of needing little or no ironing. Sheeting is very wide, so joins are not necessary, and it is available in a large range of pastel and strong colours, both plain and patterned.

4 Divide the sides and bottom edge of the panel into six equal sections and mark with pins. Pull up the gathering stitches in each frill section until it fits the corresponding panel section. Pin each section in place with the right sides of the fabric facing.

Stitch the frill in place 1.5 cm (½ in) from the raw edge. Stitch again close to the first line of stitching and neaten the raw edges by machine zigzagging over them. Press the seam allowance towards the panel. Turn a double 1 cm (½ in) hem along the remaining raw edges of both the frill and panel. Pin and stitch.

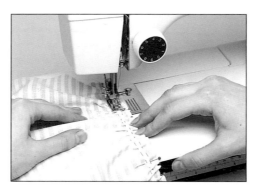

RIGHT Crisply checked pillowcases and duvet cover accentuate the light and airy feel of a country-style bedroom.

4 Turn so that the wrong sides are facing. Make a French seam around the remaining three sides, as follows. Pin and stitch 5 mm (¼ in) from the raw edge. Trim the seam close to the stitching, then open the fastener and turn the cover so that the right sides are facing. Stitch around the three sides again to enclose the raw edges and complete the seam. Turn the cover to the right side.

Most of the manufacturers listed here supply their products to good independent retailers, major stores and DIY multiples. Try your local outlets first; they will usually be able to help you and can be found in the area business directory. If you have difficulties in obtaining specific items, contact the relevant company head office for more information.

TOOLS AND BASIC MATERIALS

Black & Decker Ltd *Power tools* Westpoint, The Grove, Slough, Berkshire SL1 1QQ, UK. 0753 511234

General Woodwork Supplies (SN) Ltd *Timber, tools and hardware* 76–80 Stoke Newington High St, London N16 5BR, UK. 071-254 6052

Gripperrods plc *Carpeting tools and accessories* Wyrley Brook Park, Walkmill Lane, Bridgtown, Cannock, Staffordshire WS11 3XA, UK. 0922 417777

Hobbs & Co Ltd *Builders Merchants* 88

Blackfriars Road, London SE1 8HA, UK. 071-928 1891

Mosley Stone *Painting and decorating tools* Wellington Road, Leeds LS12 1DU, UK. 0532 630221

Plasplugs Ltd *Tiling tools* Wetmore Road, Burton-on-Trent, Staffordshire DE14 1SD, UK. 0283 30303

Stanley Tools *Woodworking, Painting and decorating tools* Woodside, Sheffield S3 9PD, UK. 0742 768888

Whincop & Son Ltd *Timber and builders merchants* 32/40 Stoke Newington Church St, London N16 0LU, UK. 071-254 5044

Allway Tools Inc *Hand tools* 1255 Seabury Avenue, Bronx, New York, New York 10462, USA. (212) 792 3636

Black & Decker *Power tools* Communications Department, 702 East Joppa Road, Towson, Maryland 21286, USA

Robert Bosch Power Tool Corporation *Power Tools* 100 Bosch Blvd, New Bern, North Carolina 28562, USA

Home Building & Lumber Co Inc *Lumber* 1621 Ave H, Rosenberg, Texas 77471, USA. (713) 342 4282

Skil Corporation *Tools* 4300 West Peterson Avenue, Chicago, Illinois 60646, USA

Stanley Tools *Woodworking, painting and decorating tools* 1000 Stanley Drive, New Britain, Connecticut 06053, USA

Seco Tools Canada Inc *Hand tools* Mississanga, Ontario, Canada. (416) 568 4080

Parburyss Building Products *Wood merchants* 30 Bando Road, Springvale, Victoria 3171, Australia. (03) 547 9033

H J Reece Pty Ltd *Hand tools* 2 Barney Street, North Parramatta, NSW 2151, Australia. 008 01 8606 (toll free)

Stanley Works Pty Ltd *Woodworking, painting and decorating tools* PO Box 10, 400 Whitehorse Road, Nunawading, Victoria 3131, Australia

Wreckair Pty Ltd *Power tools* 2 Chisholm Road, Regents Park, NSW 2143, Australia. (02) 645 4000

Nees Hardware Ltd *Tools* 11–15 Pretoria Street, Lower Hutt, New Zealand

Stanley Tools (NZ) Ltd *Woodworking, painting and decorating tools* PO Box 12-582, Penrose, Auckland, New Zealand

Tuf Tools CC *Woodworking, painting and decorating tools* PO Box 212, Maraisburg 1700, Transvaal, South Africa

PAINTS & WOOD FINISHES

Laura Ashley Ltd 150 Bath Road, Maidenhead, Berkshire SL6 4YS, UK. 0628 770345

Cuprinol Ltd Adderwell, Frome, Somerset BA11 1NL, UK. 0373 465151

Crown Paints Crown House, Hollins Road, Darwen, Lancs BB3 0BG, UK. 0254 704951

Dulux (ICI plc Paints Division) Wexham Road, Slough, Berkshire SL2 5DS, UK. 0753 550000

Arthur Sanderson & Sons Ltd 100 Acres, Oxford Road, Uxbridge, Middx UB8 1HY, UK. 0895 238244

Builders Square Inc *Decorating store* 9725 Datapoint Drive, San Antonio, Texas 78229, USA. (512) 616 8000

Wilson W A & Sons Inc *Decorating store* 6 Industrial Park Drive, Wheeling, WV 26003, USA. (304) 232 2200

Dulux Australia 145 Cabarita Road, Concord, NSW 23137, Australia. (02) 736 5111

Pascol Paints Australia Pty Ltd PO Box 63, Rosebery, NSW 2018, Australia. (02) 669 2266

Sikkens (Tenaru Pty Ltd) PO Box 768, Darlinghurst, Sydney, NSW 2010, Australia. (02) 357 4500

Taubmans 51 McIntyre Road, Sunshine, Victoria 3020, Australia. (03) 311 0211

ICI Hutt Park Road, PO Box 30749, Lower Hutt, New Zealand

Taubmans (New Zealand) Ltd 10 Portsmouth Road, PO Box 14064, Kilbirnie, Wellington, New Zealand. 0800 735 551 (toll free)

Dulux (Pty) Ltd 8 Juyn Street, Alrode, PO Box 123704 Alrode, South Africa

WALL COVERINGS

Laura Ashley (*see Paints*)

Crown Berger Ltd (*see Paints*)

Forbo–CP (Fablon) Ltd Station Road, Cramlington, Northumberland NE23 8AQ, UK. 0670 718300

Forbo–Kingfisher Ltd Lune Mills, Lancaster, Lancashire LA1 5QN, UK. 0524 65222

Harlequin Wallcoverings Ltd Cossington Road, Sileby, Nr Loughborough, Leicestershire LE12 7RU, UK. 0509 816575

Monkwell Fabrics and Wallpapers 10–12 Wharfdale Road, Bournemouth, Dorset BH4 9BT, UK. 0202 752944

Arthur Sanderson & Sons Ltd (*see Paints*)

Muriel Short Designs Hewitts Estate, Elmbridge Road, Cranley, Surrey GU6 8LW, UK. 0483 271211

Today Interiors Hollis Road, Grantham, Lincolnshire NG31 7QH, UK. 0476 74401

Crown Wallcovering Corp 20 Horizon Boulevard, South Hackensack, New Jersey 07606, USA. (201) 440 7000

Mazer's Discount Home Centers Inc *Decorating store* 210 41st Street S, Birmingham, Alabama 35222, USA. (205) 591 6565

Pratt & Lambert Inc *Decorating store* 75 Tonawanda Street, Buffalo, New York 14207, USA. (716) 873 6000

North American Decorative Products Inc 1055 Clark Boulevard, Brompton, Ontario, Canada L6T 3W4

Davro Interiors 616 Hay Street, Holimont, WA 6014, Australia. (09) 387 4888

International Paints Birmingham Avenue, Villawood, NSW 2163, Australia. (02) 728 7577

TILES

The Amtico Company Ltd *Vinyl tiles* 1177 St George Street, London W1R 9DF, UK. 071-629 6258

Castelnau Tiles *Wall and floor tiles* 175 Church Road, Barnes, London SW13 9HR, UK. 081-741 2452

Corres Mexican Tiles *Ceramic wall tiles* 219–221 Chiswick High Road, London W4, UK. 081-994 0215

Fired Earth Tiles plc and **The Merchant Tiler** *Ceramic, terracotta, stone and slate tiles* Twyford Mill, Oxford Road, Adderbury, Banbury, Oxfordshire OX17 3HP, UK. 0295 812088/812179

H & R Johnson Tiles Ltd *Ceramic floor and wall tiles* Highgate Works, Tunstall, Stoke-on-Trent ST6 4JX, UK. 0782 575575

Daniel Platt Ltd *Natural clay products* Brownhill Tileries, Canal Lane, Tunstall, Stoke-on-Trent ST6

4NY, UK. 0782 577187

Westco Ltd *Vinyl, cork and wood-block floor tiles* Penarth Road, Cardiff, South Glamorgan CF1 7YN, UK. 0222 233926

Wicanders (GB) Ltd *Cork floor and wall tiles* Stoner House, Kilnmead, Crawley, West Sussex RH10 2BG, UK. 0293 527700

American Olean Tile Company 1000 Cannon Avenue, Lansdale, Pennsylvania 19446, USA. (215) 855-1111

Armstrong World Industries PO Box 3001, Lancaster, Pennsylvania 17603, USA. (800) 233-3823

Crossville Ceramics Box 1168, Crossville, Tennessee 38557, USA. (615) 484-2110

Latco Tiles 2948 Gleneden Street, Los Angeles, California 90039, USA. (213) 664-1171

Summitville Tiles Inc Box 73, Summitville, Ohio 43962, USA. (216) 223-1511

Greenbank Tertech Pty Ltd *Ceramic tiles* 5 Hereford Street, Berkeley Vale, NSW 2259, Australia. (043) 88 4522

Bruce Floor (Vic) Pty Ltd *Linoleum tiles* 60 Punt Road, Windsor, Victoria 3181, Australia. (03) 51 5222

FLOOR COVERINGS

Crucial Trading Ltd *Natural floor coverings* 4 St Barnabas Street, London SW1, UK. 071-730 0075

Forbo Nairn Ltd *Cushioned vinyl and linoleum* PO Box 1, Kirkcaldy, Fife, Scotland DY1 2SB. 0592 261111

Heuga UK Ltd *Carpet tiles* The Gate House, Gate House Way, Aylesbury, Buckinghamshire HP19 3DL, UK. 0296 393244

Junckers Ltd *Hardwood strip flooring* Wheaton Court Commercial Centre, Wheaton Road, Witham, Essex CM8 3UJ, UK. 0376 517512

Kosset Carpets Ltd Tofshaw Lane, Bradford, West Yorkshire BD4 6QW, UK. 0274 681881

Tomkinsons Carpets Ltd PO Box 11, Duke Place, Kidderminster, Worcestershire DY10 2JR, UK. 0562 820006

Westco Ltd *Wood-block floor tiles* (see Tiles)

Woodward Grosvenor & Co Ltd *Carpets* Stourvale Mills, Green Street, Kidderminster, Worcestershire DY10 2AT, UK. 0562 820020

Kentile Floors Inc 58 Second Avenue, Brooklyn, New York, New York 11215, USA

Stark Carpet Corporation 977 Third Avenue, New York, New York 10022, USA

Dorsett Carpet Mills Inc 502 11th Avenue, Dalton, Georgia 30721, USA. (706) 278 1961

ETC Carpet Mill Ltd 3100 S Susan Street, Santa Ana, California 92704, USA. (714) 546 5601

Bruce Floor (Vic) Pty Ltd *Carpets* (see Tiles)

Carpet and Decor Centre 26 Central Road, Fordsburg 2092, Johannesburg, South Africa. (011) 833 2311

FEATURES & FITTINGS

J D Beardmore & Co Ltd *Architectural hardware* 3–4 Percy Street, London W1P 0EJ, UK. 071-637 7041

Richard Burbidge Ltd *Timber mouldings, shelving and fire surrounds* Whittington

Road, Oswestry, Shropshire SY11 1HZ, UK. 0691 655131

Fireplace Designers Ltd *Fire surrounds and accessories* 157c Great Portland Street, London W1N 5FB, UK. 071-580 9893/4

Harrison Drape *Curtain poles and accessories* Bradford Street, Birmingham B12 0PE, UK. 021 766 6111

Hodkin & Jones (Sheffield) Ltd *Decorative plaster mouldings* Callywhite Lane, Dronfield, Sheffield S18 6XP, UK. 0246 290888

Fixture Hardware Co Inc 4711 N Lamon Avenue, Chicago, Illinois 60630, USA. (312) 777 6100

Handy Hardware Wholesale Inc 8300 Tewantin Drive, Houston, Texas 77061, USA. 97130 644 1495

SOFT FURNISHINGS

Laura Ashley Ltd (see Paints)

Forbo–Kingfisher Ltd (see Wall Coverings)

Harlequin wallcoverings Ltd (see Wall Coverings)

Monkwell Fabrics and Wallpapers (see Wall Coverings)

Arthur Sanderson & Sons Ltd (see Paints)

Muriel Short Designs (see Wall Coverings)

Today Interiors (see Wall Coverings)

Decor Home Fashion Inc 140 58th Street, Brooklyn, New York 11220, USA. (718) 921 1030

Southwest Quilted Products Inc 18100 Kovacs Lane, Huntington Beach, California 92648, USA. (714) 841 5656

North American Decorative Products Inc (see Wall Coverings)

Tissus Rosedale Inc D'Anjou, Quebec,

Canada. (514) 351 8402

Nichimen Australia Ltd 3rd Floor, 60–70 Elizabeth Street, Sydney, NSW 2000, Australia. (02) 223 7122

STORAGE

Addis Ltd Ware Road, Hertford, Hertfordshire SG13 7HL, UK. 0992 584221

Cliffhanger Shelving Systems 8 Fletchers Square, Temple Farm Industrial Estate, Southend-on-Sea, Essex SS2 5RN, UK. 0702 613135

MFI Southon House, 333 The Hyde, Edgware Road, Collingdale, London NW9 6TD, UK. 081-200 0200.

Silver Lynx Products Ltd Lynx House, 10/11 Amber Business Village, Amber Close, Tamworth, Staffordshire B77 4RP, UK. 0827 311888

Spur Shelving Ltd Otterspool Way, Watford, Hertfordshire WD2 8HT, UK. 0923 226071

Shelves & Cabinets Unlimited 7880 Dunbrook Road, San Diego, California 92126, USA. (619) 578 4200

Bernhard Woodworking Ltd Inc 3670 Woodhead Drive, Northbrook, Illinois 60062, USA. (708) 291 1040

Caringbah Sheet Metal (Aust) Pty Ltd 42 Cawarra Road, Caringbah, NSW 2229, Australia. (02) 524 0791

Algoran Shelvit (Pty) Ltd Botha Street, Alrode, Alberton, South Africa. (011) 640 864 3900

SUNDRIES

Concord Lighting Ltd Alton House, High Holborn, London WC1, UK. 071-497 1400

Ideal-Standard Ltd *Bathroom equipment, furniture and accessories* PO Box 60, National Avenue, Hull HU5 4JE, UK. 0482 46461

Mazda Lighting Miles Road, Mitcham, Surrey CR4 3YX, UK. 081-640 1221.

Oracstar Limited *Plumbing and ventilation products* Weddell Way, Brackmills, Northampton NN4 0HS, UK. 0604 702181

Philips Lighting Ltd PO Box 298, City House, 420/430 London Road, Croydon, Surrey CR9 3QR, UK. 081-665 6655